THE HIGH ALTITUDE BAKER

RECIPES FOR ALPINE BAKING

Audrey Harty

Storyteller Books, LLC

To all the people at home during COVID-19 taking this time to bake.

CONTENTS

MOUNTAIN SPECIALTIES

FOREWORD

Successful baking requires three steps:

- Accurate measurements
- Thorough mixing
- Proper doneness

Pay careful attention to these three aspects, and you will achieve beautiful baked goods, treats, and desserts—most of the time.

In this book, Audrey guides you to successful baking with detailed descriptions of her experiences baking from sea level to 8,500 feet of elevation in the Wasatch Mountains. The lessons she's learned are here for you to apply to your baking.

Audrey has always been a conscientious person. Growing up, she was very diligent with her school work, working hard to do the best she could with each project or assignment. This would often lead to long hours spent on schoolwork while classmates had finished, yet Audrey would persevere. From an early age, she showed self-discipline and thoughtful planning.

She created recipes as soon as we would let her cook. Writing down the exact way she liked her quesadillas made (including spices and cooking times), testing her guacamole ratios of lime, garlic, salt, and cilantro to make it just right. She'd make adjustment notations in the Joy of Cooking, questioning new flavor profiles for old favorites and taking pride in baking to her satisfaction. That, so many years ago, was the start of this creative effort.

Determined before 20 years of age to not pay rent, Audrey purchased her first home at age 21 (before she got her driver's license, but that's another story).

In middle school, her interest in creating art, ceramics, and good food led to a career in professional bakeries. Audrey got a job at 15, serving fondue and chopping apples at Deer Valley Ski Resort. Her introduction to the culinary field, starting as a "Baker's Assistant," gave her experience in both cooking and baking. She wasn't discouraged by long hours of standing or working evenings and weekends.

Audrey has an adventurous soul. From skateboarding and breakdancing, skiing (way too fast for her mother) and surfing, rock climbing, and sailing. Her adventures in culinary travel have exposed her to new ideas, flavors, and experiences that have guided her taste and creativity.

Whether Cascade Culinary school in Bend, OR., chocolate production in Hawaii, street bazaars in Mexico City, working at a winery in the Loire Valley, France, dining her way through Paris, New York, Minneapolis, San Francisco, Norway, and Denmark, have all added to her culinary know-how.

Determined to learn, she can be a bit forward in asking questions like "What's that spice in there?" or "How did you get the texture like this?" to staff at restaurants and bakeries. She dines for pleasure as well as knowledge.

Audrey's worked in professional kitchens starting as a bakers assistant, bakery counter attendant, where she would prep and explain desserts to the guests, and a production baker (learning the three aspects of successful baking). Then onto lead baker roles for banquets and restaurants, inspiring other bakers with her (some would say perfectionist) quest for excellent baked goods. Audrey was promoted to Pastry Chef at the Goldener Hirsch hotel as well as Chocolatier for Deer Valley Resort due to her constant desire to be a better baker.

The insights in this book are Audrey's way to make you—The High Altitude Baker—comfortable with the differences in baking at altitude. A culmination of her determination and curiosity that will help you with your baked goods.

Stephen J Harty (Loving Father)
Former Executive Pastry Chef

INTRODUCTION

Welcome to life at 7,000 ft in Park City, Utah. I've lived in the Wasatch Mountains my whole life, and I've enjoyed baking since childhood. My other love is traveling, whether it's to another mountain community or a rustic European village, traveling never gets old.

The best part is always the food and pastries. The recipes I'm sharing with you come from a wide array of sources: friends, previous jobs, family, and even people I met on my travels. When I noticed I'd collected recipes from so many different people and places, it was time to make them into a cookbook.

These recipes will give you confidence in high altitude baking. The title refers to you. You are the high altitude baker, not me. I am just the chef and author and teacher. There is a section on the science of high altitude baking to help you apply adjustments to any recipe you want to make, expanding beyond those I'm sharing with you.

The recipes are all written for baking at 6,500 ft to 8,500 ft altitude. But they all include adjustments for baking between sea level and 4,000 ft. If you live between those altitudes, make your adjustments to in between what's suggested.

Baking requires precision and patience. And those traits are even more important in the mountains. Baking requires more specialized equipment than cooking does. Below are two lists of equipment used in this book.

Tools you will need for most of these recipes:

- digital scale
- electric mixer
- measuring cups and spoons
- rubber spatula
- whisk
- mixing bowls
- sheet pan or two
- parchment paper

- most of all, patience

Less common tools that some recipes use:

- cake pan
- loaf pan
- muffin pan
- ice cream machine
- food processor
- chocolate mold
- saucepan
- food thermometer (preferably digital)
- zester/microplane

See the back of the book for measurement conversion charts.

WHAT MAKES BAKING AT HIGH ALTITUDES DIFFERENT?

The answer is in some science, physics mostly. The higher the elevation, the less air pressure. This affects three things:

- Boiling temperature is lower
- Moisture evaporates faster
- Gasses expand faster

We must counter these effects to make the same delicious desserts created at sea level. The air is drier in the mountains. You may need to add water or remove flour from recipes. There are no hard rules for changing recipes with changes in altitude. But here are a few guidelines.

For recipes of cookies and cakes from sea level follow the chart below:

Cake Adjustment Guide				
Ingredient	10,000ft+	10,000ft-8,500ft	8,500ft-6,500ft	6,500ft-3,500ft
Sugar Decrease each cup/7oz by:	3+ Tablespoons	2-4 Tablespoons	1-3 Tablespoons	0-2 Tablespoons
Baking Soda or Baking Powder Decrease each teaspoon	1/2-2/3 teaspoon	1/4-1/2 teaspon	1/8-1/4 teaspoon	1/8teaspon
Flour Increase each cup/5oz by	2-4 Tablespoons	3-4 Tablespoons	0-2 Tablespoons	0-1 Tablespoon
*Water based liquid Increase each cup/8oz by:	3+ Tablespoons	3-4 Tablespoons	2-4 Tablespoons	1-2 Tablespooons

When making candy or caramel, decrease 2 degrees Fahrenheit for every 1,000 ft in elevation you climb. Caramel point at sea level is 320-335F. So for 7,000 ft, reduce the final temperature by 14 degrees Fahrenheit from a sea-level recipe, and you'll get caramel at 306-321F.

Boiling temperature at sea level is 212F. It goes down 2 degrees Fahrenheit for every 1,000 ft you go up. This means if you're high in the Andes of Ecuador, your pasta will take longer to cook because your water may only be 190F. It also means your crème anglaise is going to take longer, and your apple pie filling may need to be precooked to have the right balance of doneness in your crust and apples.

If you're baking yeast-based breads, start with a little less flour than the recipe calls for. Try to proof in a cool environment so the bread can expand at a slower rate. Also, try reducing the yeast a little. Every bread recipe is different, and there is no formula. I recommend finding a recipe written for baking at high altitude, perhaps in my next book.

COOKIES

Cookies are one of the desserts that are most affected by a change in altitude. Spreading into each other. Leaking butter all over. Crisp as caramel. We've all been there.

What happens is as the air pressure reduces the higher you go, water evaporates faster, concentrating the amount of sugar in the cookies. Too much sugar equals cookies as thin as crepes and as crispy as a potato chip. The gasses from the baking soda and baking powder expand faster: creating small volcanoes inside your oven.

The solution is simple: reduce the sugar and the leavening agents. In some cookie recipes, you may want to increase the flour and add a tablespoon of water. Again, there is no hard rule since the science behind each cookie recipe is different.

If you ever want to try a cookie recipe in the mountains made for sea level, you'll need to experiment with "educated trial and error." Start by decreasing sugar by 1 Tbsp per cup/7oz for every 4,000 ft. Reduce baking soda and baking powder by 1/8 tsp per 1 tsp for every 5,000 ft.

RECIPES:

Alfajores (Dulce de Leche Sandwiches)
Dulce de Leche
Diego's Mexican Wedding Cookies
Grandma's Chocolate Chip Cookies
Walnut Thumbprint Cookies
World Peace Cookies

ALFAJORES

ou may have heard of *Alfajores*, or at least *dulce de leche*.
These cookies are a traditional South American and
Central American cookie. Like many recipes, they vary
widely from region to region. But they are always filled with *dulce de
leche*. Leche is Spanish for milk, and *dulce de leche* is caramelized milk.

I asked for this recipe from my former coworker, Florencia, after she handed out cute bags of her own *Alfajores* to her baker friends. She had a small sweets business back home in Paraguay. She was kind enough to share her precious recipe with me and let me share it with the world.

This version is gluten-free, due to cornstarch only instead of a combination of cornstarch and flour. Still, the texture is just as buttery and tender as any delicious cookie should be. Actually, having no gluten allows you to reroll the dough as many times as necessary to cookie cut it all and not overwork it.

Just because they are traditionally filled with pure dulce de leche does not mean you have to limit yourself to that, as you will see below. But in this case, you can't go wrong with a classic.

Dough Ingredients:
  3.5 oz Butter, soft
  2.8 oz Powdered Sugar
  5 Egg Yolks
  1 tsp Vanilla Extract
  8.8 oz Corn Starch
  1 tsp Baking Powder
  3 Tbsp Powdered Milk
  ⅛ tsp Salt

Filling Ingredients:
  8 oz Dulce De Leche (see below for homemade recipe)
  3 oz White Chocolate
  as needed Fine Shredded Coconut
  as needed Semisweet chocolate

Yield: 68 1 ¼" sandwiches or 2lb 11oz of dough

Mixing Time: 20 minutes
Rolling and Cutting Time: 20 minutes
Baking Time: 15-20 minutes
Tools Needed: Digital scale, measuring cups and spoons, rubber spatula, electric mixer and bowl, rolling pin, sheet pans, parchment paper, double boiler, piping bag (best but not necessary).
Pro Tips: If you want them to stay gluten-free make sure your powdered milk is not malted.
If you want it to be dairy-free as well as gluten-free, eliminate the milk powder. Replace the butter with a dairy-free substitute, and make a dairy-free chocolate or white chocolate ganache filling.
If you buy dulce de leche, make sure to read the ingredients and that it has no corn syrup in it. You can find the best quality at a Latin food grocery store, but it is also in most grocery stores in the baking section.
Altitude Adjustments: None

Alfajore Dough:

1. Whisk together cornstarch, baking powder, and powdered milk in a bowl and set aside.
2. Using an electric mixer, cream butter and powdered sugar together.
3. Mix in egg yolks and vanilla, scraping the sides and bottoms occasionally.
4. On low speed mix in dry ingredients.
5. Preheat oven to 210F
6. On a cornstarch dusted surface, roll to a quarter inch thick. Then cut to 1 ½" diameter (or preferred size) with a cookie cutter. If you don't have a cookie cutter, get creative, use a shot glass or lid of some sort.
7. Bake 15 minutes or until they can be slid around on the pan and some have cracks in the top.
8. For traditional Alfajores, fill with dulce de leche and roll

sides in fine shredded coconut or dip in melted chocolate. For a less traditional style you can pick any filling and decoration of your choice.

9. I find that in warm places the dulce de leche oozes a little too much, so I mix it with some white chocolate to make a dulce de leche ganache that is stiffer.

10. For the dulce de leche and white chocolate ganache mix 3 oz white chocolate to 4 oz dulce de leche melt over a double boiler and stir. Chill in an ice bath, stirring frequently, until a pipe-able consistency. Store at room temperature or in the fridge. You will have extra ganache.

HOMEMADE DULCE DE LECHE

Ingredients:
One 14oz can Sweetened condensed milk

Yield: 1 ¼ Cups
Time: 2+ hours, mostly passive
Tools Needed: Small and large deep baking pan, aluminum foil.
Altitude Adjustments: None

1. Heat oven to 425°F with rack in the middle.
2. Pour the contents of 1 (14-ounce) can of sweetened condensed milk into a 9-inch deep-dish pie plate or similar baking dish and cover tightly with foil.
3. Set plate in a larger pan and add enough hot water to the pan to reach 1 inch up the sides. Be careful of steam when you open the oven.
4. Bake milk in middle of the oven for 45 minutes. Check water level and add additional, if necessary, then continue to bake 1 hour more, or until milk is thick and brown. The

dulce de leche will thicken more as it cools. In this case darker is better because thicker is better. Aim for a milk chocolate brown.

5. Remove pie plate from water bath and cool, uncovered.

DIEGO'S MEXICAN WEDDING COOKIES

*T*hese are similar, *but not exactly* like the cookies we think of when we hear Mexican Wedding Cookies, Pecan Sandies, or Russian Tea Cakes.

Traveling in Veracruz with my fiancé, we stopped in to visit my friend and former workmate Diego Noriega Manez. After Diego finished his internship in Park City, he returned home to Mexico and started his own bakery.

We had the privilege to try most of his pastries, his homemade pasta, and lasagna. I saw these long cookies with a pecan in the center and asked if they were Mexican wedding cookies. Diego snickered and informed me that Mexican wedding cookies didn't exist in Mexico.

He explained that these were the closest cookies to the American version of Mexican wedding cookies. While they are occasionally served at Mexican weddings—they were not strictly for weddings.

I love dipping these in a cup of coffee in the morning, like I would with a biscotti, and eating them.

Ingredients:
    10.5 oz All Purpose Flour
    7 oz Butter, soft
    1.5 oz Granulated Sugar
    1.5 oz Brown Sugar
    1 Whole Egg
    1 Egg Yolk
    1/8 tsp Almond Extract
    ½ tsp Salt
    ⅜ tsp Baking Soda
    1 Cup Pecans, finely chopped
    Pecan Halves

Yield: 24-30 cookies
Time: 1 hour
Tools Needed: Electric mixer, spatula, whisk, sheet pan, parchment paper, french knife, and a digital scale.
Pro Tips: If your butter is cold when you start, warm it in the

microwave with a cup of water next to it, in 20 second intervals. Flip the butter over after the first two intervals. The process minimizes meltage.

Altitude Adjustments:

Sea level-4,500 ft: Increase granulated sugar to 2 oz, baking soda to ½ tsp, and change eggs to 2 yolks, no white.

10,000 ft+: Decrease baking soda to ½ tsp and butter to 6.5 oz.

1. Preheat your oven to 325F
2. Mix butter and sugars until creamy.
3. Add eggs and extract. Mix, scraping the bottom occasionally.
4. Whisk flour, salt, and baking soda together in a bowl.
5. On low speed, add the flour mixture and mix until just combined, then mix in the chopped pecans.
6. Scoop into heaping-tablespoon sized balls and roll into a football shape (American football).
7. Flatten and round the ends, then press a pecan half in the center of each one.
8. Place on a parchment lined pan 1" apart and bake until golden around the edges, about 12 minutes.
9. Enjoy by dipping in a warm cup of coffee or milk.

GRANDMA'S CHOCOLATE CHIP COOKIES

I couldn't have a cookie section without a chocolate chip cookie recipe. I've worked with many chocolate chip cookie recipes in the professional kitchens, but this one is made for home bakers.

My grandma Adrienne's cookies are so popular that she makes them in batches of 40 at a time. I give my grandmother credit for me going into the baking and pastry industry. She is an excellent cook, baker and a significant reason my father became a pastry chef.

My grandmother lives in Minnesota in the summer and Florida in the winter. This recipe was made initially for baking between sea level and 1,000 ft. I have adapted it for alpine baking, and like all recipes, I've included adjustments for baking at lower altitudes.

Ingredients:

2 ¾ Cups All Purpose Flour
¾ tsp Baking Soda
1 tsp Salt
8 oz (2 sticks) Unsalted Butter, melted
½ Cups Granulated Sugar

¾ Cups Brown Sugar, packed
2 tsp Vanilla Extract
1 Tbsp Milk
2 Eggs
13 oz Chocolate Chips

Yield: 40 3" cookies
Time: 1 hour-1 hour 20 minutes
Tools Needed: Electric mixer, digital scale, measuring cups and spoons, rubber spatula, sifter, sheet pan, parchment paper, cooling rack.
Pro Tips: Soften your butter by warming in the microwave with a cup of water next to it at 20 second intervals, rotating every time, until soft.
Altitude Adjustments:
Sea level-4,000ft: Decrease flour to 2 ¼ Cups, increase baking soda to 1 tsp, increase granulated sugar to ¾ Cup, and decrease milk to 1 tsp. Bake at 375F for 5 minutes.
10,000 ft+: Reduce baking soda to ½ tsp and remove 2 tsp from the sugar.

1. Prepare pans with parchment paper and set the oven to 365F.
2. Sift together flour, baking soda, and salt.
3. Beat together butter and sugars until well combined.
4. Beat in eggs, scraping the bowl before and after.
5. On low speed mix in the flour mixture until just combined. Scrape the sides and bottom.
6. Mix in the chocolate chips, but don't over mix.
7. Scoop to the size of two level tablespoons.
8. Bake at 365F, checking after 8 minutes. Take out when light brown. Leave on the hot pan for 5 more minutes before transferring to a cooling rack. This makes chewy rather underdone cookies.

9. Store in an airtight container.
10. If you're not going to eat 40 cookies in the next few days, store some of them in the freezer for baking at a later date, or store baked cookies in the freezer for future consumption.

WALNUT THUMBPRINT COOKIES

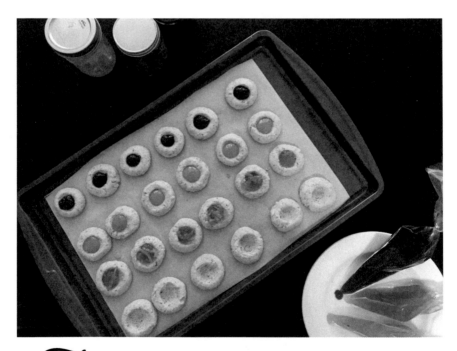

his recipe originated from culinary school in Bend, Oregon (one of my favorite places in the US). I had never thought of including nuts in thumbprint cookies. To me, they were more of a traditional shortbread cookie, perhaps a little sweeter than that, often including almond extract, but not nuts.

Then I tasted them with almond flour, and it was a revelation. In one of my classes, the final was to create a plated dessert with four elements learned from that term. My dessert was walnut based. I processed walnuts as fine as possible without making walnut butter. Which is why we add flour to the food processor, to keep it dry. I liked them more than the almond ones. Feel free to replace the walnuts with other nuts or even almond flour.

As for the fruit preserves in the photo, the raspberry jam comes from my local organic grocery store, the passion fruit jam comes from my summer in Hawaii where tropical fruits are abundant. The lemon-vanilla marmalade was a gift from my friend and fellow pastry chef Tim Snyder right before he moved to San Francisco.

Ingredients:
  1 ½ Cups (5.3 oz) Walnuts
  ½ Cup All Purpose Flour
  1 Cup All Purpose Flour
  ⅛ tsp Salt
  6 oz Unsalted Butter, softened
  1 Cup Powdered Sugar
  2 Egg Yolks
  1 tsp Vanilla Extract
  ¼ tsp Almond Extract
  1 Cup Raspberry, Strawberry, Apricot, or other fruit jam.

Yield: 50 cookies
Prep Time: 25 minutes
Mixing Time: 10 minutes
Baking and Cooling Time: 25 minutes
Tools Needed: Food processor (or sharp chef's knife), electric mixer,

measuring cups and spoons, rubber spatula, whisk, 2 sheet pans, parchment paper, piping bags, or spoons.

Pro Tips: You can chill your dough and use it later, but it's best when it's still room temperature and very soft because pressing your finger into a cold ball of dough will cause more cracks in your cookies.

Altitude Adjustments:

Sea level-4,500 ft: Increase powdered sugar by 1 tablespoon.

1. Preheat your oven to 325F and line a sheet pan with parchment paper.
2. Place nuts in your food processor with the ½ Cup of flour. If you do not have a food processor, you can chop the nuts to the finest consistency you can (without the flour) this will cost you 20 extra minutes.
3. Add remaining flour and salt and pulse until nuts are reduced to a powder.
4. Beat butter until just smooth. On low-speed mix in powdered sugar.
5. Mix in the yolks and extracts, scraping several times until combined.
6. Add the nut and flour mixture to the mixer. Mix on low speed until combined. Your dough will be very soft.
7. Scoop each cookie to the size of 2 level teaspoons or ⅔ of a level tablespoon. (**When I say teaspoon and tablespoon here, I mean measuring spoons, not silverware.**)
8. Roll each scoop into a ball. Press your finger ⅔ into each cookie. Press together any cracks so there will be no leakage. Laying them out just over an inch apart. I fit 4 by 6 on my pans.
9. Bake on a parchment-lined tray until the cookies are set and can slide on the parchment when nudged. About 12 minutes.
10. Meanwhile, pull out your jam or jams of choice. If you have piping bags, that is the easiest way to fill them, but you can

also just use two spoons: one to scoop, one to move jam from spoon to cookie.

11. Remove the cookies from the oven. Repress the indent into your cookie before filling if necessary. Fill each one with about 1 tsp of the preserves.

12. Return to the oven and bake until lightly browned on the bottom and a skin has formed on top of your jam. 5-7 minutes.

13. Remove from the oven and cool on the pan for 5 minutes before eating. Store in an airtight container at room temperature for up to 5 days.

14. Dust with powdered sugar for garnish if desired.

WORLD PEACE COOKIES

These cookies were invented by French pastry chef, Pierre Herme. He shared them with his friend and associate Dorie Greenspan. She made them famous by putting them on the cover of her book Dorie's Cookies.

I was introduced to them working at Deer Valley, where they were called "chocolate obsession cookies." They are one of my favorite cookies in the world, if not my number one favorite. That little bit of salt on top, the buttery goodness, and the melty chocolate chunks really make them irresistible.

While still good the second day, or baked and stored frozen, world peace cookies are genuine heaven in a cookie half an hour after they come out of the oven. You can mix a batch and keep your logs of raw dough in the freezer, then slice and bake at your convenience. Perfect for a last minute treat to bring to a party, or a shameless personal pleasure. The dough will last for months in the freezer.

Ingredients:
  2.3 oz Cocoa Powder
  12 oz All Purpose Flour
  1 tsp Baking Soda
  ½ tsp Salt
  22 oz (2 ¼ sticks) Unsalted Butter, softened
  8oz Brown Sugar
  3.5 oz Granulated Sugar
  1 tsp Vanilla Extract
  11oz Bittersweet Chocolate, chopped (60%-75%)
  Fleur de Sel or other mild sea salt.

Yield: 72 Cookies
Prep Time: 40 minutes
Bake Time: 12 minutes
Tools Needed: Electric mixer, rubber spatula, sifter or fine sieve, measuring spoons and cups, scale, sheet pan, parchment paper, french knife.
Pro Tips: This is a shortbread recipe, meaning you are aiming for

tender and buttery. To achieve that you want to mix as little as possible, so you don't develop too much gluten.

Altitude Adjustments:

Sea level-5,000 ft: Increase brown sugar to 8.5 oz.

10,000 ft+: Reduce granulated sugar to 3 oz and baking soda to ¾ tsp.

1. Preheat your oven to 325F
2. Sift the cocoa powder into a bowl to get rid of clumps, whisk in the flour, baking soda, and salt.
3. In an electric mixer beat the sugars and butter together
4. Mix in the vanilla extract
5. On low-speed mix in the dry ingredients until only just combined.
6. Add the chopped chocolate and mix until evenly distributed.
7. Split the dough in half and roll into 1 ½" logs, then chill for 3 plus hours.
8. Slice into ½" slices. Your dough may break on some of the slices. Just press the pieces back together to create a disk.
9. Place on a parchment-lined sheet pan with 1" between each cookie.
10. Sprinkle a few crystals of the fleur de sel or mild salt on the top of each cookie.
11. Bake for 12 minutes on the middle rack. They will not appear done, but they will be.
12. Remove the pan from the oven and let it cool for 5 to 10 minutes. Then, using a flat spatula, transfer them to a cool platter or pan.
13. Serve within the next 8 hours for the best experience.

BREAKFAST PASTRIES

Quick breads and muffins follow similar guidelines to cakes when it comes to alttitude adjustments.

The way chemically leavened products work is by applying moisture and heat to your baking soda, or baking powder to produce carbon dioxide. The carbon dioxide forms bubbles within the glutenous walls of your batter. The proteins in the flour and eggs are what build structure in muffins, quick breads, and cake. Sugar and fat weaken the cell structure.

The decreased air pressure above 3,500 ft allows the gasses created by the leavening agents to expand rapidly, stretching the cell structure too far, breaking it. You end up with collapsed muffins, quick bread, or cake. Adding on to the cells being stretched to their breaking point, the increased water evaporation concentrates the sugar, which weakens the structure, and takes flavor out of balance.

For further information see the cake adjustment chart in the "What Makes Baking At High Altitude Different" section.

RECIPES:

Chocolate Zucchini Bread
Citrus Muffins
Grandma's Banana Bread
Home Made Granola
Pistachio Mountain Rolls
Easy Home Made Croissant Dough
Sesame Seed Muffins

CHOCOLATE ZUCCHINI BREAD

I love the way the grated zucchini makes this bread so moist that you barely even need butter to enjoy it. And the chocolate just makes it.

Ingredients:
   3 oz Cream Cheese, room temp
   8.8 oz (1 ¼ Cups) Granulated Sugar
   2 Eggs
   ⅓ Cup Canola Oil
   1 ½ tsp Vanilla Extract
   10 oz All Purpose Flour
   1.5 oz Cocoa Powder
   1 ½ tsp Cinnamon
   ¾ tsp Baking Powder
   ¾ tsp Baking Soda
   ¾ tsp Salt
   1 ½ Cups (8 oz) Zucchini, grated
   4.5 oz Chocolate Chips
   ¾ Cups Sliced Almonds, or nut of choice, plus some for garnish

Yield: One 9" loaf pan or 1 smaller loaf pan plus a few muffins
Prep and Mixing Time: 1 hour
Baking Time: 1 to 1 ½ hours
Tools Needed: Digital scale, measuring cups and spoons, rubber spatula, electric mixer, mixing bowl, medium bowl for dry ingredients, sifter, whisk, box grater, 9 ½" by 5" loaf pan or muffin tin and papers,
Pro Tips: Don't over mix your batter at any stage.
Altitude Adjustments:
Sea level to 4,500 ft: Bake at 350F for 55 to 70 minutes. Increase sugar to 1 ½ Cups. Reduce vanilla to 1 tsp. Increase baking powder to 1 tsp. Increase baking soda to 1 tsp. Lining the sides of the pan with parchment is not necessary, just the bottom plus spraying the whole pan.

1. Spray loaf pans with baker's spray and line bottom and long sides with parchment paper.
2. Grate Zucchini.
3. Measure dry ingredients in a bowl. Set aside.
4. Beat cream cheese and sugar in an electric mixer.
5. Preheat your oven to 375F.
6. Add eggs one at a time, scraping frequently.
7. Add oil and vanilla.
8. Sift dry ingredients, then whisk together.
9. Add dry ingredients to the wet mixture.
10. Stir in Zucchini, chocolate chips, and nuts.
11. Fill your loaf pan ⅔ full, bake any excess batter in paper lined muffin tins, also filled ⅔ full. Sprinkle garnish nuts on top and bake for 60-75 minutes. First 15 minutes 375F, then turn down to 350F for 25 minutes, then rotate and turn down to 325F, then check every 15 minutes for doneness. If the crust on top is baked but the insides are still raw, tightly cover with a piece of aluminum foil.
12. Your bread is done when a paring knife comes out clean and the internal temp is over 203F.

13. Cool for 20 minutes before removing from the pan. To remove from the pan, run a knife around the edges and pull on the paper to loosen before flipping over. Cool to 100F internal temp before serving or cool all the way before wrapping. Store at room temp for up to a week or in the fridge for up to three weeks.

CITRUS MUFFINS

*T*o me poppyseeds don't have a strong enough flavor to complement the lemon and orange zest in this recipe, so I've replaced them with finely chopped toasted almonds.

You can toast some almond flour and use it as a substitute, but starting with sliced almonds allows you to keep some crunch by not grinding them all the way to a powder.

Ingredients:
⅔ Cup Sugar
1 Tbsp Lemon Zest, packed
2 Tbsp Lemon Juice
1 Tbsp Orange Zest, packed
1 Tbsp Orange Juice
2 ¼ Cups All Purpose Flour
1 tsp Baking Powder
⅛ tsp Baking Soda
¼ tsp Salt
¾ Cup Sour Cream
2 Large Eggs
1 ½ tsp Vanilla Extract
½ Cup or 1 stick Unsalted Butter, melted
¼ Cup Sliced Almonds, toasted and finely chopped

For the Icing
1 Cup Powdered Sugar, sifted
2 Tbsp Lemon Juice
1-2 Tbsp Water

Yield: 12 muffins
Prep Time: 25 minutes
Bake Time: 15 to 20 minutes
Tools Needed: Zester, rubber spatula, whisk, measuring cups and spoons, mixing bowls, muffin pans, muffin papers, citrus juicer, pastry brush.
Pro Tips: If you don't have a juicer, just use a pair of tongs to pinch the citrus fruit, but make sure you don't get any seeds in the muffins. Avoid overmixing this recipe. We melt the butter for that exact

reason. Overmixing will make these muffins less tender and fluffy and more tough and bouncy.

Altitude Adjustments:

Sea level-4,000 ft: Reduce flour to 2 cups, increase baking powder to 2 tsp, increase baking soda to ¼ tsp, and reduce vanilla to 1 tsp.

8,500-11,000 ft: Reduce baking powder to ¾ tsp and sugar by 1 Tbsp. Start oven at 350F and turn down to 325 when you put the muffins in.

Batter and Baking:

1. Preheat your oven to 325F. Line your muffin pan with paper liners.
2. Zest and juice your lemon and orange. Mix the zests and sugar together until a wet sand consistency and the sugar has taken on some color from the oils.
3. Toast the almond slices. Let them cool, then chop until very fine, but not a powder.
4. Turn the oven up to 400F
5. Melt the butter.
6. Whisk your eggs until frothy, then mix in the sour cream, juices, and vanilla extract.
7. While stirring, pour in your butter. The egg and sour cream mixture is cold, so the butter will solidify when it makes contact. You are trying to prevent large chunks from forming.
8. Whisk your dry ingredients together, including the chopped almonds.
9. Add the sugar to the wet mixture, and mix until combined.
10. Stir in the flour mixture until you see no more flour, then stop. There may be a few lumps, but just like in pancake batter, that's fine.
11. Fill the muffin papers to ½ inch from the top and smooth the tops of the batter if wonky. Bake until tops color slightly

with golden spots and a paring knife inserted in the center of a center muffin comes out clean, about 15 to 20 minutes.

Finishing:

1. Meanwhile, prepare the glaze. In a small bowl melt the butter, then mix in the powdered sugar and lemon juice.
2. Right after you pull the muffins out of the oven brush them with the glaze, use up all the glaze. Transfer the muffins to a cooling rack.
3. These muffins are best the day they are baked, but can be kept frozen for up to two months.
4. If you eat them in the next few days, rewarm in the oven at 325 or in the microwave for 20 second intervals until steaming.

GRANDMA'S BANANA BREAD

Another delicious recipe from my grandma Adrienne in Minnesota. Growing up, we visited my grandparents and family in Minnesota and Wisconsin every summer. I could always count on there being banana bread, bagels, and freshly cut fruit upstairs in the kitchen in the morning.

I would go straight for the banana bread, cut two slices, warm it up in the microwave, and spread a little butter on each slice. I'd put a few pieces of cantaloupe on my plate and go help my sister with the daily crossword puzzle. I hope the scent of this bread brings back such fond memories for you and your family.

Ingredients:
⅓ Cup Butter, soft 2.7oz
¾ Cup 2 Tbsp Granulated Sugar
2 Eggs
3 Large Ripe Bananas, mashed
1 ½ Cups All Purpose Flour
½ tsp Baking Soda
½ tsp Salt
⅔ Cup Chocolate Chips (optional)

Yield: One 9" loaf pan
Time: 2 hours
Tools Needed: Electric mixer, rubber spatula, measuring cups and spoons, loaf pan, parchment paper, paring knife.
Pro Tips: For a more tender texture don't over cream your butter sugar and egg mixture, but don't under mix it either.
Altitude Adjustments:
Because water evaporates faster at high altitude, quick breads can lose their moisture too fast, which concentrates the sugar too much. This can cause the surface of the bread to cook too quickly, and reduce structure inside, resulting in collapse. In order to counter that we reduce the sugar and leavening, and add an extra egg for structure and moisture. If the surface of your bread is still getting too hard and dark before the center cooks you can place aluminum foil on top, shiny side down.
Sea level-4,000 ft: Increase granulated sugar to 1 Cup. Increase baking soda to 1 tsp. Decrease to 1 egg.

1. Spray 2 small loaf pans very well on sides and bottom and line with parchment paper. Set your oven to 350F.
2. Cream together first 3 ingredients
3. Add remaining ingredients
4. bake about 40-50 minutes, but check after 30 minutes. Try not to overbake.
5. If your bread is getting too hard on the surface wrap in aluminum foil.
6. Test for doneness with a paring knife.
7. Cool for 5+ minutes in the pan before removing.
8. Once fully cool store in plastic wrap or other airtight casing.

HOMEMADE GRANOLA

Ingredients:

1 lb (5 Cups) Rolled Oats
3.5 oz Sesame Seeds
4.5 oz Pecans or Walnuts, chopped

4.5oz Almonds, sliced
4.5 oz Pumpkin Seeds
4 oz Sunflower Seeds
2 ½ tsp Cinnamon
¾ tsp Ginger
1 ½ tsp Kosher Salt
2 Tbsp Canola oil
2 Tbsp Flaxseed oil
¾ Cup 1 Tbsp Honey
½ Cup 2 Tbsp Maple Syrup
6 to 7 oz Dried Fruit, chopped if large

Yield: 6 to 8 Cups
Time: 90 minutes at high altitude, 1 hour at lower altitudes.
Tools Needed: Digital scale, measuring cups and spoons, rubber spatula, sheet pans.
Pro Tips: If you do not have flaxseed oil, you can use coconut oil, hemp oil, grapeseed oil or more canola oil instead, adding up to a total of ¼ Cup of oil. The goal is equal amounts of omega-3 fatty acids and omega-6 fatty acids. Omega-3s burn easier, so the canola oil balances that, but omega-3s are often lacking in the western diet. This cookbook is no health food book, and this recipe has a lot of sugar, but even a little difference helps. For an even healthier recipe, add ¼ Cup of wheat bran or oat bran; stir it into your liquid before adding to the bowl of dry ingredients.
Altitude Adjustments:
Sea level-5,000 ft: Decrease baking time to around 1 hour.

1. Preheat your oven to 325F.
2. Measure all of the ingredients ahead of time. Dried fruit in one bowl, liquids in a small saucepan, mix remaining dry ingredients in a large bowl.

3. Bring the oil, honey, and maple syrup to a boil. Do not cook once boiling or you will burn the sugars.
4. Once the liquids have reached a boil, pour them over the dry and mix until fully incorporated.
5. Transfer the mixture into sheet pans or hotel pan, and bake, stirring at 10-15 minute intervals, until golden brown. Break up clumps as it cools.
6. Mix in the dried fruit and store in an airtight container or package in bags.

PISTACHIO MOUNTAIN ROLLS

Photo by Steve Harty

I went to culinary school in Bend, Oregon. A wonderful town full of breweries, bakeries, rock climbing, one of my favorite ski resorts—Mount Bachelor, and endless other forms of outdoor recreation.

A local bakery there, The Sparrow Bakery, is famous for its ocean roll dessert. I loved it so much I made my own version. Their recipe is a well-kept secret, so this one is from trial and error.

I knew they used house-made croissant dough, and the main flavor is cardamom, one of my favorite spices. So mountain rolls have croissant dough and cardamom, they also have vanilla bean, salt, and my personal addition, toasted pistachios. Mmm. As long as you're not allergic to nuts, I promise you won't regret trying these.

You can use store bought croissant dough, but make sure you buy it in sheet form from the frozen section, not the canned stuff that doesn't even have real butter of yeast.

EASY HOMEMADE CROISSANT DOUGH:

Ingredients:
    4 Cups All Purpose Flour
    ¼ Cup Granulated Sugar
    3 ½ tsp Instant Yeast
    2 ⅛ tsp Kosher Salt
    1 ¼ Cups Unsalted Butter, cold (2 ½ sticks)
    1 Cup Milk, Whole, 2% or Almond (you may need an extra table-spoon or two)

Yield: Twelve 4" Mountain rolls, or 8 rolls plus 6 croissants
Dough Time: 2 hours
Filling and Assembly Time: 40 minutes
Proofing and Baking Time: Overnight + 30 minutes
Tools Needed for dough: Large bowl, wooden spoon, measuring cups and spoons, knife, cutting board, rolling pin.
Tools Needed for Filling and Assembly: Whisk, paring knife, sheet pan, french knife.
Pro Tips: Instead of a fresh vanilla bean for your sugar mix, you can use the vanilla sugar from the *vanilla ice cream recipe*. If you use a fresh vanilla bean with this recipe, use the rind to make more vanilla sugar

or your own vanilla extract. Vanilla beans are expensive, so get as much as you can out of them.

Try using the croissant dough recipe for traditional croissants. Roll the dough out to a 10" wide rectangle, ⅛" thick. Cut into triangles, 5 inches at the wide end, and tightly roll up. Proof and bake under the same instructions below.

Altitude Adjustments:

Sea level-5,000 ft: Increase yeast to 4 tsp. Increase salt to 2 ¼ tsp. Increase oven temp to 375F and bake for a shorter time. The internal temp of your dough only needs to be 190F.

Croissant Dough:

1. Slice your butter into ⅛" thick squares
2. Mix your dry ingredients together in a bowl, then toss the butter in it until coated.
3. Pour the milk in and stir until it comes together as a stiff dough.
4. Knead into a solid dough ball.
5. Wrap and chill for half an hour.
6. On a floured surface, roll the dough into a long rectangle shape.
7. Fold it into thirds like a letter.
8. Rotate 90 degrees and repeat folding into thirds and rolling out 4 to 6 times, or until chunks of butter have turned into streaks and you can see thin layers of butter and dough when you slice through it. Be careful not to make too many folds or it will all blend together, and you will lose that layered flakiness.
9. If the butter ever starts to feel soft, or the dough won't stretch anymore, chill it in the fridge for 30 minutes, then continue the folding process.
10. Chill for one more hour then roll into a 14" by 15" rectangle for assembly.

Photos by Steve Harty

FILLING AND ASSEMBLY:

Ingredients:
¾ Cups Chopped Pistachios, lightly toasted
½ Cup Granulated Sugar
⅔ Vanilla Bean
1 ½ tsp Cardamom
1 pinch Salt (unless your pistachios are salted)
as needed Egg wash
as needed Coarse Sugar or Demerara Sugar

1. While the dough is chilling, mix together the sugar, cardamom, salt, and the insides of the vanilla bean. Rub it between your fingers to separate vanilla seeds.
2. Lightly brush or spray the dough with egg wash. Leaving a 1" gap at the edge of the dough for sealing shut. Spread the sugar mixture evenly on the dough. Evenly sprinkle the toasted pistachios on top.
3. With the 14 inch sides on the left and right, roll the dough forward into a tight log.
4. Slice to 3.5 ounce pieces and flatten with your palm into a 1" thick circle.
5. In a professional kitchen, I place these in a 4" entremet ring sprayed before proofing, but these can be proofed and baked freeform as well.
6. Proof in a warm humid space until puffy and the dough does not spring back when pressed with a finger. If you do not have a proofer, lightly spray the surface with water, and lay a damp towel over the top, elevate the towel with some upside-down cups. Then place in a sunny spot, checking every half hour.
7. 10 minutes before it's ready preheat your oven to 365F.
8. Apply egg wash, then sprinkle generously with coarse sugar or demerara sugar and then finely chopped raw pistachios.

9. Bake until golden brown and feels very light when lifted. Check with a thermometer in a layer of bread only for 195F to make sure there is no raw dough inside.
10. Around 30 minutes at 7,000 ft elevation, 15 to 20 minutes at lower altitudes.

SESAME SEED MUFFINS

*A*n unusual but delicious recipe. These are sweet but not too sweet. And while intended for a yummy sweet breakfast you can enjoy them as a side for a savory dish like corn muffins.

When I created this recipe, I wanted to include a tried and true lemon poppyseed recipe. But I decided *a* lemon *poppyseed muffin recipe was too boring*. I thought, *what about a sesame seed muffin recipe? Ooh, yeah, that sounds really good.*

And this recipe was born, created by blending other recipes I had in my collection. No safe but classic lemon poppyseed muffin recipe in this book, instead, something more adventurous and equally delicious.

Ingredients:
    ¼ Cup Sesame Seeds, toasted
    2 Eggs
    1 Cup Vegetable Oil
    ⅛ tsp Sesame Oil
    ¼ tsp Almond Extract
    1 Cup (8oz) Evaporated Milk
    1 ¼ tsp Vanilla Extract
    1 Cup (7oz) Granulated Sugar
    2 tsp Baking Powder
    ¼ tsp Salt
    1 ½ Cups All Purpose Flour
    ¼ Cup Sesame Seeds, untoasted

Yield: Eighteen 2 ½" diameter muffins
Mixing Time: 30 minutes
Baking Time: 30-35 minutes at 7,000 ft
Tools Needed: Large bowl, rubber spatula, measuring cups and spoons, whisk, sheet pan, muffin pans, muffin papers.
Pro Tips: When toasting the sesame seeds stir or toss often in the pan.
Altitude Adjustments:
Sea level-5,000 ft: Increase baking powder to 1 Tbsp. Increase granulated sugar by 1 Tbsp. Baking time may be less.

1. Preheat the oven to 350F.
2. Toast the first measurement of sesame seeds in a dry pan on the stove on medium heat until rich in color and aroma. Careful not to overcook them and leave a bitter taste. Taste test once cool.
3. Whisk the dry ingredients (except sesame seeds) together in a bowl.
4. In a separate bowl, whisk the eggs until frothy. Whisk in the rest of the wet ingredients.
5. Add toasted sesame seeds to liquid ingredients to stop the cooking. It may sizzle when you dump them in.
6. Combine all ingredients, except for the final sesame seeds, in a mixing bowl and whip until thoroughly combined.
7. Pour into lined muffin tins. Sprinkle the final sesame seeds on top and bake for 30 minutes.
8. They are done when a small knife comes out clean, and they are bouncy when lightly pressed.
9. Cool for 5 minutes then remove from the pan to cool the rest of the way, or serve warm with butter.
10. Store in an airtight container in the fridge for up to a week. Rewarm and butter before eating for best experience.

ICE CREAMS AND SORBET

Anglaise Not Ready: Anglaise ready

Altitude doesn't affect the making of ice creams, sorbets, and the like. Sugar percentage is what makes frozen desserts stay soft, or semi-frozen. Just like saltwater freezes at a lower temperature, so does sugar-water. It has to do with density.

To get liquid to freeze just enough but not too much, it must have a sugar percentage between 15 and 30 percent. Ice cream, which has the addition of fat, needs less sugar, between 15-25% and sorbet 20-30%. Unless you add alcohol, which is another anti-freezing agent.

If you ever make an ice cream or sorbet recipe and it freezes too hard after churning, melt it and add a tablespoon or two of alcohol. Make sure you melt the ice cream in the fridge for food safety purposes.

What can affect sorbets, is if too much water evaporates at high altitude when cooking the liquid. Water evaporates at a lower temperature, the higher you go. The more water that evaporates, the higher the sugar percentage, the softer your sorbet will be.

At lower altitudes, Anglaise may take as little time as five minutes to reach its proper viscosity. The higher up you are, the longer it will take. The longer it's on the heat, the lower the final temperature will need to be because your eggs are cooking toward coagulation for longer.

RECIPES:

Ice Cream Cones
Hibiscus sorbet
Pistachio Gelato
Toasted oat ice cream
Oat Crumble (Streusel)
Vanilla bean ice cream
Vanilla Sugar

ICE CREAM CONES

$\mathcal{T}$hink of making ice cream cones like making pancakes or crepes, because that's what they are. This is a waffle cone recipe made into cones without a waffle cone iron. If you happen to have a waffle cone iron, feel free to use this recipe with it.

It took practice to figure out temperature and timing with cooking and shaping this delicious classic cookie. I'd start with a double batch if it's your first time. Remember to have patience. Patience is often the most important ingredient in baking.

Ingredients:
    2 Egg Whites
    ½ Cup Granulated Sugar
    3 Tbsp Milk, lukewarm
    1 Tbsp Butter, melted
    1 Stick of Butter for greasing your pan
    ½ tsp Vanilla Extract
    1 pinch Salt
    ⅔ Cup All Purpose Flour

Yield: Eight 6" tall cones
Prep Time: 12 minutes
Cook Time: 8 minutes per cone
Tools Needed: Offset spatula (recommended) or rubber spatula and flipping spatula, bowl, whisk, measuring cups and spoons, nonstick pan or cast iron griddle, cooling rack.
Pro Tips: A pan with low or no edges will be easier when spreading the batter and lifting and flipping the disk. I use butter on my pan just like the French do when making crepes, but you can also use cooking spray if you wish.
This recipe is also great for homemade fortune cookies, just look up a guide on how to shape them and voila!
Altitude Adjustments: None

1. Whisk the egg whites and sugar together until foamy.
2. Warm your milk in the microwave until lukewarm, then melt your butter.

3. Mix in the rest of the ingredients and whisk until foamy.

4. Heat your griddle or nonstick pan to medium heat and coat a 7" circle with butter or cooking spray. Spoon 1 ½ tablespoons of batter onto the hot pan and quickly spread into an even 6" circle with a mini offset spatula. This will take practice, but you can do it!

5. Allow to cook until golden brown on one side, about 4-6 minutes, then run your spatula under it, pressing firmly against the pan so as not to tear the cookie. Flip over and cook for another 1-2 minutes. Remove from heat and quickly shape. The moment it comes off the heat it will begin to stiffen. Use a towel to protect your hands if the cone is too hot.

6. Start by forming the point. Fold in half with the smooth side on the outside and pinch one end. Overlap the flaps keeping the pinched end in a point and the other end a wide opening. Hold until your cone will hold its shape on its own, place on a cooling rack, then start the next one. Make sure to clean your spatula and rebutter the pan in between uses.

7. Use right away or store in an airtight container in a dry place for up to 3 days. Alternatively, the batter can be stored in the fridge for several days.

HIBISCUS SORBET

The first time my fiancé and I went to Mexico was to Puerto Escondido, Oaxaca. It was October, and unbearably hot on the coast. I'm not made to be at sea level, the mountains will always be my home.

Due to the heat, we had lots of cold icy drinks, and that is how I discovered *jamaica*. Spelled just like the country Jamaica, jamaica is a word in Spanish pronounced huh-my-kuh.

Jamaica is a beverage made of steeped hibiscus petals and sugar, then chilled and served in a tall glass with lots of ice. Hibiscus is exceptionally tart. It needs lots of sugar added to it, which is great for sorbets. For a sorbet to not be too soft or too hard, it must have the right percentage of sugar, 20 to 30 percent.

Photo by Cecelia McCarty: Glass of Hibiscus sorbet made Granité style

Ingredients:
   3 Cups Water
   ½ Cup Hibiscus Petals, dried

⅛ tsp Salt
⅓ Cup Honey
⅔ Cup Granulated Sugar
1 tsp Powdered Pectin

Yield: 1 Quart.
Making the Base: 40 active minutes. 90 passive minutes.
Freezing in an Ice Cream Machine: 15-30 minutes depending on your machine.
Freezing Granité Style: 4-5 hours
Tools Needed: Medium saucepan, ice cream machine*, measuring cups and spoons
Pro Tips: You can find hibiscus petals in your local Latin grocery store or online, just make sure it is hibiscus petals only, not a mixed tea. The pectin helps make for a smoother sorbet. Most sorbets are made with fruit, which naturally has pectin in it, some fruits more than others such ass apples, peaches and guavas. Pectin is a setting gelling agent used most often for making jams and jellies.
Altitude Adjustments:
Sea level-3,000 ft: Reduce water by 1 Tbsp.
10,000 ft+: Increase water by 2 Tbsp.

| Ingredients | Steeping the petals |
| Straining the tea | The honey has been dissolved |

1. Measure ingredients.
2. Place water, hibiscus petals and salt in a saucepan and bring to a boil.
3. Turn heat down and simmer for 10 minutes.
4. Turn off heat and steep until the petals have absorbed enough water to sink, then your tea is properly infused. 5-10 minutes

5. Pour through a fine mesh strainer and press as much liquid out of the petals as you can.

6. Place 3 Cups of the tea back in the pot and add the honey, sugar and pectin. Heat on medium stirring occasionally until the honey, sugar and pectin are all dissolved, and the liquid is homogeneous. About 8 minutes.

7. Mix in with the rest of the tea. This makes it so the honey, sugar and pectin do not get absorbed by the petals and you have the same amount of sugar crystals with every batch.

8. Place in a glass container and chill until cold to the touch. About 90 minutes. Don't use plastic, it will cause off-flavors.

9. Churn according to instructions on your ice cream machine.

Variation: If you don't have an ice cream machine, you can make this sorbet granité/granita style. A fancy way of saying place the liquid in a glass or metal container in the freezer and stir every 30 minutes while the ice crystals form for 4-5 hours. You will not get the smooth texture of sorbet, more of a shaved or flaky ice texture, but delicious and scoopable. (The dessert in the photo was made with this technique.)

LINGONBERRY ICE CREAM

*W*hen I was the pastry chef at the Goldener Hirsch Inn at Deer Valley, the chef wanted me to make a lingonberry dessert. Lingonberries were trendy at the time. I decided on a chocolate cake, mousse filling and a mirror glaze accompanied by this tart ice cream to complement the chocolaty richness.

Lingonberry Puree Ingredients:
    12 oz Lingonberries
    ¼ Cup Water
    ¼ tsp Salt
    2 Tbsp Water

Ice Cream Base Ingredients:
    1 ½ Cups Heavy Cream
    1 ½ Cups Whole Milk
    1 Cup Granulated Sugar
    1 ¼ Cup Lingonberry Puree

Yield: 4 ½ Cups
Active Time: 25 minutes
Total Time: Up to 8 hours
Tools Needed: Ice cream maker, blender/food processor, digital scale, medium saucepan, measuring cups and spoons, rubber spatula, whisk, mixing bowl.
Pro Tips:
Taste the batter before churning, if it is too tart for you add another tablespoon of sugar, but don't add too much more or your ice cream will be too soft when done.
Make sure to not let the puree cook to the bottom of the pan, scrape it every few minutes with a spatula.
Altitude Adjustments:
10,000 ft+: add 2 tablespoons of water to the saucepan.

Lingonberry Puree:

1. Combine berries, water and salt in a medium saucepan and cook on medium heat for 6-7 minutes.
2. Remove from heat and cool for 10 minutes.
3. Puree the cooked berries and water in a blender or food processor until well pureed.
4. Refrigerate until cold. Alternatively, place in the freezer and stir often until cold.

Ice Cream:

1. Whisk the heavy cream, milk, sugar and puree together.
2. Churn according to your ice cream machine's instructions to soft serve consistency.
3. Transfer to a chilled ice cream container.

4. Freeze for 4 to 6 hours before serving. May need to thaw for a few minutes before scooping.

Variation: Replace part or all of the lingonberries with cranberries. Cranberries have nearly the same flavor as lingonberries, perhaps a little more bitter. They are both tart, and this recipe applies to both. Cranberry ice cream makes a great Thanksgiving dessert but can be enjoyed at any time of year.

PISTACHIO GELATO

*G*elato is the Italian word for ice cream. It starts out with a similar custard base as ice cream, but has a higher proportion of milk and a lower proportion of cream and eggs (or no eggs at all). It is churned at a much slower rate, incorporating less air and leaving the gelato denser than ice cream.

Ingredients:
   ¾ Cup Unsalted Shelled Pistachios, toasted (about 3 ¾ ounces)
   ¾ Cup Granulated Sugar
   2 Cups Whole Milk
   1 Cup Heavy Cream
   1 pinch Salt
   ¼ tsp Almond Extract
   5 Large Egg Yolks
   2 Drops Green Food Coloring (optional)
   as needed Chopped Pistachios, salted and toasted

Yield: 1 Quart

Ice Cream Base: 1 hour active + 4 hours passive

Churning and Freezing: 15-30 minutes + 4 hours passive

Tools Needed: Food processor, measuring cups and spoons, medium saucepan, rubber spatula, whisk, thermometer, sieve, wooden spoon, ice bath, ice cream machine.

Pro Tips: Aging the base, refrigerating overnight, is more important for custard-based ice cream than cream-based or vegan ice creams. It results in more robust flavors and a creamier texture. However, it is not 100% necessary.

Altitude Adjustments: At lower altitudes, the anglaise may take as little time as five minutes to reach its proper viscosity, but the higher up you are the longer it will take. The longer it's on the heat, the lower the final temperature will need to be, because your eggs are cooking toward coagulation for longer.

1. Finely grind first pistachios and ¼ Cup of sugar in the food processor.
2. Combine pistachio mixture, milk, heavy cream and salt in a heavy medium saucepan. Bring to boil.
3. Prepare an ice bath.
4. Whisk yolks and remaining ½ Cup of sugar together in a large bowl.
5. Whisking constantly, slowly pour half of the hot cream mixture into the egg yolks to temper them. Return the liquid to the saucepan.
6. Stir over medium-low heat until custard thickens slightly and leaves a path on the back of a spoon when a finger is drawn across (170-180F). Do not boil.
7. Remove from heat and pour into a container in an ice bath. Whisk in Almond extract and food coloring.
8. Refrigerate overnight.
9. Churn according to instructions on your ice cream machine. It's done when it holds its shape when a spoon is dragged through, and very slowly relaxes.

10. Transfer to an airtight container and freeze for at least 4 hours.
11. Scoop into glasses or bowls. Garnish with chopped, salted, toasted pistachios.

TOASTED OAT ICE CREAM

Infused Milk Ingredients:

2 lb 7 oz Whole Milk
7 oz Toasted oats

Ice Cream Base Ingredients:

1 lb 13 oz Infused Milk
5 oz Heavy Cream
½ tsp Cinnamon
3.5 oz Granulated Sugar
3 oz Egg Yolks

Oat Streusel/Crumble Ingredients:

6 Tbsp All Purpose Flour
6 Tbsp Brown Sugar
¼ Cup Oats
½ tsp Cinnamon
3 Tbsp Butter, cold
2 pinches Salt

Yield: 1 ½ Quarts
Ice Cream Base: 1 hour active + 4 hours passive
Churning and Freezing: 15-30 minutes + 4 hours passive
Oat Crumble Time: 15 minutes
Tools Needed For Ice Cream: Digital scale, sheet pan, parchment paper, measuring cups and spoons, medium saucepan, rubber spatula, thermometer, sieve, whisk, wooden spoon, cheese cloth, ice cream machine.
Tools Needed For Oat Crumble: Knife, cutting board, measuring spoons and cups, electric mixer or pastry blender, sheet pan, parchment paper
Pro Tips: Make sure not to let the oat milk steep too long, oats absorb liquid, and you will not have enough milk if it sits too long. If you don't have enough steeped milk, just add a little more milk.
The key to a good streusel is cold butter so the flour doesn't absorb the moisture.

Altitude Adjustments: At lower altitudes the anglaise may take as little time as 5 minutes to reach its proper viscosity, but the higher up you are the longer it will take. The longer it's on the heat, the lower the final temperature will need to be, because your eggs are cooking toward coagulation for longer.

Make Infused Milk:

1. Place milk on high heat and bring to a simmer.
2. Place oats on a tray and toast for 5 minutes at 390F or until they start to have a toasted aroma (no color).
3. Add toasted oats to the warm milk. The oats must be added to the milk when both are hot for optimal infusion.
4. Take the milk off the heat and cover in plastic wrap. **Steep only for 5 minutes** so the milk doesn't thicken too much.
5. Strain through a fine sieve lined with cheese cloth if you have it.

Ice Cream Base:

1. Weigh out the necessary milk for the ice cream. If there's extra discard it, if you don't have enough just add enough non-infused milk to make the 1 lb 13 oz.
2. Heat the cream, milk and cinnamon to a simmer.
3. Whisk yolks and sugar together in a large bowl.
4. Whisking constantly, slowly pour half of the hot cream mixture into the egg yolks to temper them. Return the liquid to the saucepan.
5. Cook on medium-low heat to 170-180F. Stir constantly with a rubber spatula, making sure to scrape the bottom and sides. The custard will be thicker than a traditional anglaise due to the oats.
6. Pour the custard through a fine sieve into a container and refrigerate overnight.
7. Churn according to instructions on your ice cream

machine. It's done when it holds its shape when a spoon is dragged through, and very slowly relaxes.

8. Move into a container and place in the freezer to stiffen for at least 4 hours.

Oat Streusel:

1. Cut butter into 1/2" cubes and place in the freezer.
2. Measure out all other ingredients and mix together in a mixer bowl with paddle attachment.
3. Add the butter and mix on medium speed until the mixture starts to look like wet sand and the butter chunks are the size of small peas.
4. Chill and store in a fridge or freezer.
5. Bake at 350 for 4-8 minutes on a sheet pan lined with parchment until golden brown. Break Streusel apart or blend in a food processor to make finer crumbs.

Serve Toasted Oat Ice Cream with Oat Streusel on top.

VANILLA ICE CREAM

*W*hen I think of vanilla, I think of France and vanilla ice cream or vanilla creme brulee. But vanilla isn't from France, or Europe at all. Vanilla is native to Mexico.

The Mayans were using vanilla beans centuries before the Spanish discovered it and brought it back to Europe in the early 16th century. Vanilla is a seed pod that comes from a species of orchid that only grows in tropical environments. Just like cacao trees and coffee grow in tropical climates, but are more associated with Europe than Central America.

These are a few examples of how Europeans would bring back food from places they colonized and made their own creations from them. It was the start of what we now call food fusion.

Ingredients:
- 4 Egg Yolks
- ½ Cup Granulated Sugar
- 1 Cup Whole Milk
- 1 Cup Heavy Cream
- 1 Vanilla Bean + ¼ tsp vanilla extract or 1 Tbsp vanilla extract

Yield: 1 Quart

Ice Cream Base: 45 minutes + 4 hours-overnight

Churning and Freezing: 4 hours-overnight

Tools Needed: Medium saucepan, paring knife, measuring cups and spoons, rubber spatula, whisk, thermometer, sieve, wooden spoon, ice cream machine.

Pro Tips: Aging the base, refrigerating overnight, is more important for custard based ice cream than cream based, or vegan ice creams. It will result in stronger flavors and a creamier texture. However, it is not 100% necessary.

Altitude Adjustments: At lower altitudes the anglaise may take as little time as five minutes to reach its proper viscosity, but the higher up you are the longer it will take. The longer it's on the heat, the lower the final temperature will need to be, because your eggs are cooking toward coagulation for longer.

1. Split the bean in half lengthwise and scrape the paste out of the inside. Reserve the rind for vanilla sugar*.
2. In a small saucepan heat the milk, cream and vanilla paste over medium heat until just before it simmers. This is called scalding.
3. Prepare an ice bath.
4. Whisk yolks and ½ Cup of sugar together in a large bowl.
5. Whisking constantly, slowly pour half of the hot cream mixture into the egg yolks to temper them.
6. Pour back into the saucepan.
7. Stir over medium-low heat until the custard thickens slightly and leaves a path on the back of a spoon when a finger is drawn across (170-180F). Do not boil.
8. Pour into a container in an ice bath.
9. Churn according to instructions on your ice cream machine. It's done when it holds its shape when a spoon is dragged through, and very slowly relaxes.
10. Transfer to an airtight container and freeze for at least 4 hours before serving with your favorite dessert or on its own.

~

*VANILLA SUGAR

Tools Needed: Food processor

Vanilla sugar is great for pretty much anything that you would use normal sugar for, shortbread cookies, hot chocolate, or future ice cream making. It works great for the pistachio mountain rolls in the breakfast section.

1. Place the vanilla rind and 2 Cups of sugar in a food processor. Blend to a fine powder.

2. Store in an airtight container for at least a week to allow for infusion.
3. If the sugar has clumped together just give it another spin in your food processor before using.

Vanilla Bean Insides (Vanilla Seeds)

CHOCOLATES

Altitude does not affect chocolate work, which is nice, because chocolate involves enough science already. For fancier chocolates, you must be able to temper chocolate. In contrast to simple ganache truffles, where you only need to make ganache.

It is possible to temper chocolate by following instructions. Your chances of success are higher if you understand the science behind it. So, please, read the following pages about chocolate before proceeding to any of the recipes.

RECIPES:

Tempering Chocolate and Tempered Ganache
Paper Cornets
Chocolate Mendiants
Chile Pepper Bon Bons
Praline (Hazelnut) Truffles
Pumpkin Spice Caramel Truffles
Rosemary Olive Oil Bon Bons
Rosemary Olive Oil

TEMPERING CHOCOLATE

*C*hocolate vocabulary:

Tempering: Tempering Chocolate is the process of allowing type V

(5) crystals to multiply in the chocolate, leaving the chocolate smooth, shiny and snappy.

Blooming: When the cacao butter in solid chocolate separates out from the other ingredients, floats to the top, and crystallizes as a result of improper tempering, or coming out of temper while solid.

Ganache: Ganache is made with varying proportions of chocolate and liquid, around 50/50. Heavy cream is the most common and traditional liquid for making ganache. The more chocolate, the stiffer the ganache. Ganache can be flavored with things such as liquors, oils, zest, infusions of the cream, or spices. Many people add butter to ganaches.

Tempered Ganache: Ganache made with tempered chocolate.

Chocolate percentage: The percent of cacao solids in the chocolate. The four ingredients you will find in almost all chocolates are cocoa solids, cocoa butter, sugar, and lecithin. The darker the chocolate, the more cocoa solids.

White Chocolate: White chocolate has no cocoa solids in it. Cocoa butter is the main ingredient in white chocolate. It contains sugar, cacao butter, milk solids, and flavorings such as vanilla.

Cocoa Butter: Fat extracted from chocolate liquor by using a hydraulic press.

Chocolate liquor: A bitter liquid or paste produced when cacao beans are roasted and ground

Cacao beans: The tropical fruit from which all chocolate is made

Cornet: Paper piping bag used for decorating with chocolate, or other fine detail.

Tempering Chocolate is the process of allowing type V crystals to multiply in the chocolate.

What are type V crystals?
Chocolate has 6 types of crystals that form from the fat structure

in the cocoa butter, type I through VI. Type I melts at the lowest temperature (63F) and type VI melts at the highest temperature (97F).

There are two main ways of tempering chocolate. The first, and most common in home baking, is the seed method. You melt your chocolate to 108F then remove it from heat and stir in tempered chocolate, which is already made up of type V crystals, until it is cool enough.

The second method is the agitation method. Again, you melt your chocolate to 108F, but then you pour it onto a stone slab such as marble or granite, and quickly move the chocolate around, usually scraping with a bench knife and a putty knife. This agitates the crystals, and cools the chocolate down slowly, rather than something like sticking it in the freezer.

The constant movement has an effect of preventing type I through IV crystals from forming, and allowing type V to multiply, creating a structure that turns out smooth, and firm once completely cooled. As for Type VI crystals, they will form if you leave your solid tempered chocolate in a warm room temperature for a long period of time. The agitation method is also used in factories, but done differently. They have machines that hold the melted chocolate and vibrate while cooling it at the necessary rate, then put it in molds.

Chocolates temper at different temperatures. White chocolate is the lowest, then milk chocolate, then dark chocolate. This is because the percentage of cocoa butter changes. The more cocoa butter, the lower the temperature.

Where does altitude come into all of this? Lucky for us, it doesn't, or the difference is insignificant. The main thing about altitude that affects baking is the change in the boiling point due to lower density in the air. Since chocolate has no water in it, and chocolate melts at a temperature well below boiling point, it's pretty much the same as at sea level.

What can impact chocolate work is humidity. Humidity is your enemy. I have been working with chocolate at 7,000 ft for years, and last summer, 2019, I worked in a chocolate shop in Hawaii. They had the exact same tempering machine I had learned on in Park

City, and the process worked the same. What was so different was that Hawaii is warm and humid. Chocolate can come out of temper when kept at room temperature above 75 degrees, or not even temper in the first place. If you store it in the fridge then remove it, there can be condensation, which will ruin your temper immediately.

I know this sounds complicated, but once you've done it a few times and gain confidence, it will be second nature, and you won't even need a thermometer. Don't overthink it. Like all baking, chocolate work is a science, but in practice, it's more about technique.

Instructions for tempering chocolate with the seed method:
Have a quick read digital food thermometer or an instant read laser thermometer.

Measure your desired amount of chocolate x1.25

Start a double boiler

Add half of the chocolate to the double boiler

Scraping your bowl occasionally, bring the chocolate to the melting point or a little higher.

- Dark chocolate: 112 degrees F / 45 degrees C
- Milk chocolate: 110 degrees F / 43 degrees C
- White chocolate: 108 degrees F / 42 degrees C

Remove from the heat and add half of the remaining chocolate.
Stir continuously until these respective temperatures have been reached, adding more of the unmelted chocolate as necessary:

- Dark chocolate: 84 degrees F/29 degrees C
- Milk chocolate: 81 degrees F/27 degrees C
- White chocolate: 79 degrees F/26 degrees C

Remove any chocolate chunks that haven't melted in.
Test for doneness by dipping a metal spoon in the chocolate. If it

hardens quickly, with no chalky streaks, and a smooth shiny texture, then you have successfully tempered chocolate.

Now bring it to a holding temperature. This allows you to work with it before it solidifies, but without reheating it too much.

- Dark chocolate: 88-90 degrees F/32 degrees C
- Milk chocolate: 86-87 degrees F/30 degrees C
- White chocolate: 82-84 degrees F / 28 degrees C

If your double boiler water is still steaming, place your bowl of chocolate back on top. Don't turn the heat on. Stir and monitor the temperature. Once it's one or two degrees lower than the working temperature, remove the bowl, as the temperature will continue to rise slightly from the residual heat.

Don't let the chocolate go above the holding temperature or it will come out of temper.

Other things to avoid:
Don't let water from your double boiler get into the chocolate or it will seize, and never temper again. The cocoa solids will separate from the cocoa butter, and the chocolate will get grainy and lumpy.

When this happens, your chocolate cannot be re-tempered. Don't throw it away, save as an ingredient for something like ganache, brownies, or cake, as long as it's re-melted and mixed with another liquid.

When chocolate comes in contact with a small amount of water-based liquid, it seizes, but when mixed with a large amount of liquid, it emulsifies.

Don't let your chocolate get too hot. If heated to over 130F, the solids in the chocolate start to scorch. The result is a dry, discolored paste, with a burnt taste.

Tempered Ganache:
Made by mixing tempered chocolate with a large amount of liquid. Tempered ganache is stiffer, has a longer shelf life, keeps its smooth melty texture, and does not bring tempered chocolate out of temper when in contact.

Bon bons are the main thing I use tempered ganache for, for all of those reasons. You can fill your chocolate shells with un-tempered ganache, which is much simpler, but after a week or two your shells will bloom and become chalky in look and texture.

1. Temper your chocolate
2. Warm your liquid up to holding temperature (94F)
3. Whisk them together until smooth
4. Fill your bon bons. Note that tempered ganache solidifies much faster than basic ganache, so be quick.

MAKING A CORNET

*H*ow to make a paper piping bag, better known in the pastry world as a cornet, which translates from French to literally "horn."

Instructions: (picture guide on next page)

Step 1: Fold the Parchment and Cut. Take a square of parchment and fold it in half into a triangle. Use a sharp knife to cut into two triangles. Note that the center or the longest edge on your triangle will be the tip of your piping bag.

Step 2: Grab a Corner and Roll. With the long side facing away from you grab the right corner and bring it to the center point. Then twist it so it forms a cone.

Step 3: Bring the other corner in, wrapping it around the cone. Your points should all meet up.

Step 4: Adjust, and Tuck it in. Using your thumbs move the corners around a bit and tug on the outer flap to close the tip of the cone. Next, take all three corners and fold them ¼" in and repeat. Making sure to not let the tip of the cone open up as you do so. Now the cone should hold its shape, and you have a cornet. Congratulations!

Step 5: Fill and Use. Fill halfway full with chocolate or other pipeable substance. To close, with the seam side facing away from you, fold both corners in about half an inch, then start rolling it shut. Cut off the end of the cornet to your desired opening size. The more you squeeze out of the bag, the more you will need to roll it up.

Tip: With tempered chocolate the tip gets clogged easily, so start piping immediately after you fill the bag. If the tip does get clogged, pinch it with your thumb and forefinger to squeeze all of the partially set chocolate out. You will need to have two piping bags when working with chocolate because once the first one becomes unusable you can use the second one. Then by the time the second one has too much set chocolate, you can unfold the first one and remove the hardened chocolate from it then fold it up again and refill.

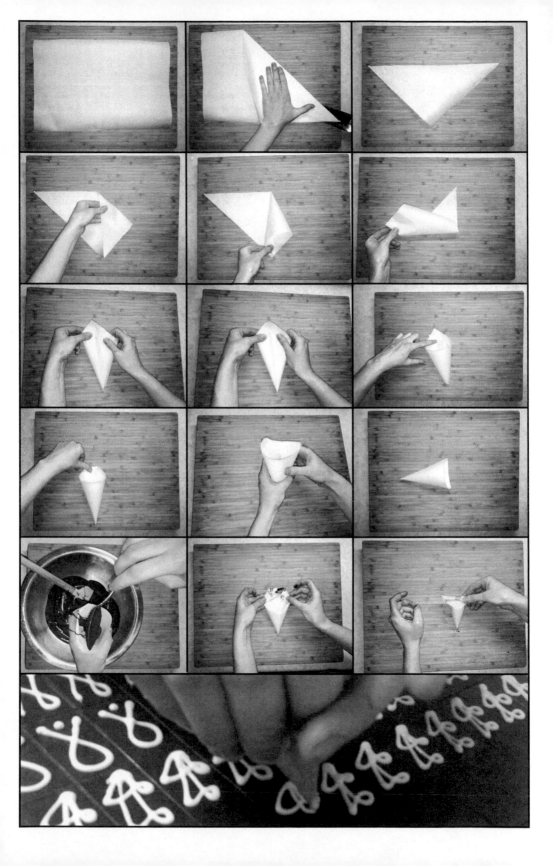

CHOCOLATE MENDIANTS

$\mathcal{C}$hocolate mendiants are a form of chocolate inclusion. Chocolate inclusions is a fancy way of saying tempered chocolate with additions such as nuts, dried fruit, spices, crushed candy, coffee grounds, or cocoa nibs.

Inclusions can be made in bar molds or free form. I was introduced to chocolate mendiants at a health fair. They were disks of tempered chocolate with a dried cranberry, a toasted pistachio, and an espresso bean on top. And that's what makes them inclusions. Whatever is "included" is just pressed in on top, not mixed in before shaping. In other words, they are simple, delicious and creative.

Ingredients:
Tempered Chocolate
Toppings: Nuts, Dried Fruit, Spices Candy, etc.

Yield: Up to you
Time: 1-3 hours depending on how many you make and if you have to toast nuts or cut fruit.
Tools Needed: Double boiler, sheet pan with parchment, spoon, cool environment.
Pro Tips: Don't let them get condensation on them.
Altitude Notes: None

1. Prepare your pan with parchment or a silpat.
2. Prepare your toppings.
3. Temper the chocolate. (See tempered chocolate page)
4. Spoon 1 ½"– 2" puddles of chocolate onto your pan, ½" apart.
5. Sprinkle/press your toppings onto the mendiants before the tempered chocolate solidifies. You may have to do this in batches, or have a helper add the toppings as you spoon the chocolate.
6. Store in a cool place.

CHILI PEPPER CHOCOLATES

*T*his recipe comes from my good friend and mentor Tim Snyder. He taught me chocolate, and got me into it. One winter at Deer Valley, he became my new pastry chef and started a chocolate production.

Tim's passion is chocolate. He had his own chocolate company when he lived in Brazil. Together we made several flavors of bonbons and created Deer Valley's own box of chocolates. This one is spicy, but chocolate and heat are a perfect pair.

Ingredients:
    Chocolate Shells:
    70% Chocolate, Double estimated volume of finished shells
    Chili Ganache:
    12 oz 70% Chocolate, Chopped
    ¾ Cup Heavy Cream
    1 Tbsp Orange Zest (about ½ an orange)
    1 Cinnamon Stick or ⅜ tsp Ground Cinnamon
    ½ tsp Red Pepper Flakes, crushed
    ⅛ tsp Salt

Yield: 20-25 bon bons
Time: 2-3 hours
Tools Needed: Double boiler, rubber spatula, measuring cups and spoons, zester, chocolate mold, sheet pan, saucepan, bench knife.
Pro Tips: The longer your cream steeps the spicier your ganache will be.
Altitude Adjustments: None

Shells:

1. Decorate chocolate molds with red and yellow dust. Best known as luster dust and found at your local baking supply store or craft store with a baking section. You can also use powdered oil based food coloring as your dust.
2. Temper your dark chocolate (see page on tempering chocolate) and use a ladle to fill the cavities in the mold.
3. Dump out onto a parchment lined sheet pan and cool the chocolate with the mold upside down, but not touching the

pan. I used a pencil at each end to prop it up; cups also work well. This is done to drain the molds so the shell is the same thickness on all sides.

4. After 3-5 minutes, when the chocolate is no longer liquid, but not totally set, scrape with a bench knife, so shells have a flat edge.

Tip: If you make bon bons often, find a chocolate that is naturally thick enough to make the shells in one layer, or add a small percentage of chocolate chips to your chocolate when you melt it. Do not use chocolate chips as your base chocolate, they are not liquid enough when melted and tempered.
Hold up to a light. If you can see any light through your chocolate, repeat the process to make thicker shells.
Tip: If you wait until the chocolate is fully set to do your second layer they will not bind together, and the shell will be fragile.

Ganache:

1. Read about tempered ganache in beginning of this chapter.

Infused Cream:

1. Pour the cream to a medium saucepan and add the orange zest, cinnamon, crushed red pepper flakes and salt.
2. Bring to a simmer.
3. Remove from heat and cover. Allow to infuse for 10 minutes.
4. Pour through a sieve to remove the pepper flakes, zest and cinnamon.
5. Cool the cream to 95F and hold there while you temper your chocolate.
6. Combine the two and fill piping bag or squeeze bottle.
7. Fill your shells ⅔ full. Try to avoid creating a nipple when pulling the ganache away, it will make the sealing process

difficult. If a small point does form, wait until the ganache has stiffened and press it down with your finger.

Ganache Variation: If you do not want to go to the trouble of making tempered ganache you can make ganache with this simple technique. However, your bon bons will not have as long of a shelf life, about 2 weeks instead of 2 months (in a cool dry environment).

1. Heat Cream to simmering.
2. Allow to infuse for 10 minutes, then strain.
3. Pour into the bowl of chocolate, let it sit for 2 minutes then whisk until homogenous.
4. Cool down to 93 degrees before filling a piping bag or squeeze bottle to fill the shells.
5. Fill the shells ⅔ full. Try to avoid creating a nipple when pulling the ganache away, it will make the sealing process difficult. If a small point does form, wait until the ganache has stiffened and press it down with your finger.

Finish:

1. Cap. Capping bon bons is the process of sealing the filling in with tempered chocolate.
2. You will need about half a cup of tempered chocolate for this, but it is easier to temper more chocolate than less chocolate, so I tempered about 1 Cup. Spoon some chocolate on top of each cavity and make sure there are no air gaps. You can leave it just like this, or you can wait until the chocolate goes a little matte looking and use your bench knife to scrape flat so when upright the chocolates have a smooth surface to sit on.
3. Place in the fridge for 15 minutes, but no more.
4. Swiftly bang on a clean cutting board or counter. Move bon

bons out of the way before banging again. If there are still any in the mold, place in the fridge for 5 more minutes, then turn upside down and tap individual cavities with a wooden spoon.

5. Store in a cool place, or in an airtight container in the fridge, bringing to room temp before opening up again to avoid condensation.

6. Enjoy!

PRALINE (HAZELNUT) TRUFFLES

*H*ave you heard of Gianduja? If you haven't, then I'm sure you've heard of NUTELLA®. Gianduja is an Italian sweet milk chocolate spread containing about 30% hazelnut paste, aka praline paste.

It's smooth, creamy, rich and nutty, and all-around delicious.

NUTELLA® was invented centuries after gianduja with the addition of palm oil as a thinner and more affordable spread, but generally the same flavor profile, if not a little sweeter.

Pretty much all nuts go well with chocolate, but, arguably, hazelnuts beat out the rest. This inspired by my love for Gianduja, and why I made this recipe.

Ganache Ingredients:

7 oz Dark Chocolate

10.5 oz NUTELLA® or 9 oz of Gianduja Spread if you don't want palm oil

½ Cup Heavy cream

Assembly Ingredients:

32 Whole Hazelnuts

1 Cup Dutch Cocoa Powder

¼ Cup Crushed and Chopped Hazelnuts

12 oz tempered chocolate (optional)

Yield: 32 truffles

Time: 1 hhur-90 minutes

Tools Needed: Digital scale, measuring cups and spoons, french knife, double boiler, paring knife.

Pro Tips: Try this recipe with home made Gianduja.

Altitude Adjustments: None

First:

1. Roast the hazelnuts in the oven at 350F until you can smell the toasty flavor (about 5 minutes), or cook on the stove in a dry pan on medium-high. Allow to cool completely

Creamy Hazelnut Ganache:

1. Melt the chocolate over a double boiler
2. Warm the cream in the microwave
3. Stir the cream and NUTELLA®)/gianduja, into the melted chocolate until combined.
4. Chill in the fridge for half an hour to an hour

Assembly:

1. Scoop the ganache with a teaspoon.
2. Roll into a ball, then flatten into a ⅛" thick circle.
3. Wrap the ganache disk around a whole hazelnut and roll in your hands to make an even ball.
4. Roll the truffles in the cocoa powder.
5. Scrape enough cocoa powder off of each truffle to expose a half-inch-sized circle of ganache.
6. Press into the chopped hazelnuts.
7. Serve.
8. For a different look, dip the truffles in tempered chocolate or just chopped nuts instead of the cocoa powder.

PUMPKIN SPICE CARAMEL CHOCOLATE TRUFFLES

I came up with this recipe while working at Hawaiian Crown Chocolate Shop in Hilo. I was blown away by how

Tom not only owned the chocolate shop, but the farm that grew, harvested, and roasted the cacao beans too.

They called it "Farm to Bar." A huge variety of cacao percentages in their chocolate bars, and several with inclusions. We had bite-sized chocolates with coconut filling, mac nuts, and caramel, but what we lacked was a proper chocolate box. The kind you give as a gift on valentines, or, if you're like me, the kind you don't want to share with anyone.

I told Tom about my past experience, showed him some pictures, and he hired me on the spot. I based this recipe on their original caramel filled chocolates, but added spices. For you home bakers, it's dipped in tempered chocolate instead of made in a mold.

Ingredients:
  ½ Cup Brown Sugar
  ½ Cup Granulated Sugar
  ¼ Cup 1 Tbsp Honey
  ½ Cup Half & half
  ½ tsp Vanilla Extract
  ¼ tsp Salt
  3 Tbsp Unsalted Butter
  ¾ tsp Cinnamon
  ½ tsp Allspice
  ¼ tsp Powdered Ginger

  2 Cups 70% Chocolate, chopped

Time: 2 hours
Tools Needed: Food thermometer, measuring cups and spoons, small saucepan, rubber spatula, 4"x 8" pan, double boiler, fork or truffle dipper, parchment paper.
Pro Tips: See page on tempering chocolate
Altitude Adjustments: At sea level sugar begins to caramelize at 270F,

but as the altitude rises and the air pressure reduces it will cook at a lower temperature. The rule of thumb is for every 1000 ft you rise, subtract 2 degrees Fahrenheit. However, this caramel is made with the half and half in with the sugars, so at 7,000 ft we cook it to about 243F.
Sea level: 257F caramel
5,000ft: 247F caramel
10,000ft: 237F caramel

Make the Caramel:

1. Combine sugars, honey, cream, vanilla, and salt in a small saucepan.
2. Heat to 243F, stirring frequently.
3. Turn off heat.
4. Add butter and spices; stir.
5. Spray pan, line with parchment, then spray parchment (or butter).
6. Pour into the pan and refrigerate.
7. Once solid cut into ½" squares, or roll into ¾" balls

Finish:

1. Temper 70% chocolate. Start with melting 1 Cup of chopped chocolate then use the rest for tempering.
2. Dip your caramel squares in the tempered chocolate with a fork and place on a tray lined with parchment. The chocolate that settles at the base of a truffle, or anything dipped in chocolate, is called the foot. Try to drain off as much of the excess chocolate as possible to reduce the foot created while it sets.
3. Garnish with a little sea salt.

ROSEMARY OLIVE OIL BON BONS

*D*on't be afraid of chocolate molds, and don't be scared to buy one or two. They are fun, affordable, and allow for more creative decoration, simple to use, and make you look cool when you share bonbons with your friends.

The above chocolates were made for Easter. I picked a mold that had an egg-like shape, and I decorated them with patterns I remember using on Easter eggs as a kid.

I got the idea for the flavor from a bakery in Mont Tremblant, Quebec. Any opportunity I get to visit a bakery when traveling is one I will take. After a few days of skiing, my fiancé and I decided to take a day to explore the town.

I went into two pâtisseries that day. The one I remember vividly was one with a showcase of the most unusually flavored chocolates. I am all about creative and unusual flavor combinations, even if they don't always sell. I mean, that's where food trends come from, right?

From most familiar to strangest, the flavors were: Strawberry, raspberry, pecan praline, cherry blossom, pistachio, honey, chili pepper, red wine, thyme and citrus, olive oil rosemary, pine sap, mustard tarragon, dijon black currant, and caramel black olive and dry tomato.

Yeah. Pretty crazy, but they were all good. The chocolatier told me that they didn't have a printed key for the chocolates because they constantly change flavors and create new ones. And that sometimes flavors turn out bad, but others are surprisingly delicious!

And that is where I got the idea for this recipe from. Then it was trial and error to make it work.

Rosemary Olive oil Ingredients:
½ Cup Rosemary Leaves, fresh
2 Cups Extra virgin olive oil, medium-strong flavor

Chocolate Shells Ingredients:
70% Chocolate, Double the estimated volume of finished shells, not fruity flavors

4 oz White Chocolate or cocoa Butter
As needed Green Food Coloring, oil based

Rosemary Olive oil Tempered Ganache:

3.5 oz Milk Chocolate, tempered
3 oz Heavy Cream, 95F
2 tsp Rosemary olive oil
1 pinch Salt

Yield: 20-25 chocolates, 2 Cups of rosemary olive oil
Average Total Time: 4 hours
Rosemary Olive oil: 10 active minutes, 20 passive.
Decorating Molds: 45 minutes
Chocolate Shells: Up to 40 minutes
Chocolate Filling: Up to 40 minutes
Capping: Up to 30 minutes
Average total time: 4 hours
Tools Needed: Chocolate mold, bench knife/dough knife, measuring cups and spoons, sheet pan, rubber spatula, piping bag.
Altitude Adjustments: None

Rosemary Olive oil:

Note: This recipe makes 2 Cups of rosemary olive oil, when for your chocolates you only need 2 tsp. Keep it in your pantry for up to a month, or fridge for 4 months. Great for dipping fresh bread in or making crostinis, adding to pasta and endless other applications. If 2 Cups is too much feel free to halve the recipe.

1. Strip the rosemary off of the sprigs, and measure. Rough chop, then slightly crush to release more flavor. A pestle or rolling pin works well.

2. Place the oil in a small saucepan and heat to 180F on medium heat. About 5 minutes.
3. Turn off the heat and add the rosemary. Steep for 20 minutes then strain out the rosemary.
4. Store in a glass or ceramic container. 10 active minutes.

Chocolate shells: While your olive oil is steeping you can decorate your shells or move on to making the shells.

1. Temper your white chocolate or cocoa butter (see page on tempering chocolate). Add food coloring a little at a time until you get a light green/yellow color. Decorate your molds in your desired design.
2. Temper your dark chocolate (see page on tempering chocolate) and fill the cavities in the mold.
3. Dump out onto a parchment lined sheet pan and cool the chocolate with the mold upside down, but not touching the pan. I used a pencil at each end to prop it up; cups also work well. This is done to drain the molds so the shell is the same thickness on all sides.
4. After 3-5 minutes, when the chocolate is no longer liquid, but not totally set, scrape with a bench knife, so shells have a flat edge.
5. *Tips: If you make bon bons often, find a chocolate that is naturally thick enough to make the shells in one layer, or add a small percentage of chocolate chips to your chocolate when you melt it. Do not use chocolate chips as your base chocolate, they are not liquid enough when melted and tempered.*
6. Hold up to a light. If you can see any light through your chocolate, repeat the process to make thicker shells. *Tip: If you wait until the chocolate is fully set to do your second layer they will not bind together, and the shell will be fragile.*
7. If you have a partner making the ganache while you make the shells then you can potentially use the same tempered chocolate for the caps before it hardens.

Olive oil Tempered Ganache:

1. Temper your milk chocolate. If milk chocolate is too sweet for you, you can add a little bit of dark chocolate to it. Ratio of 1 to 4 dark to milk. Measure your 3.5 oz of tempered chocolate in a bowl that isn't cool to the touch, or warm. I placed a cereal bowl on the stove for just a few seconds to warm it up.
2. Warm your cream to 95F
3. Add it to the tempered milk chocolate. Stir to combine.
4. Add the oil and salt. Stir to combine.
5. Transfer the ganache to a piping bag.
6. Fill your shells ⅔ full. Try to avoid creating a nipple when pulling the ganache away, it will make the sealing process difficult. If a small point does form, wait until the ganache has stiffened and press it down with your finger.

Finish:

1. Cap. Capping bon bons is the process of sealing the filling in with tempered chocolate.
2. You will need about half a cup of tempered chocolate for this, but it is easier to temper more chocolate than less chocolate, so I tempered about 1 Cup. Spoon some chocolate on top of each cavity and make sure there are no air gaps. You can leave it just like this, or you can wait until the chocolate goes a little matte looking and use your bench knife to scrape flat so when upright the chocolates have a smooth surface to sit on.
3. Place in the fridge for 15 minutes, but no more.
4. Swiftly bang on a clean cutting board or counter. Move bon bons out of the way before banging again. If there are still any in the mold, place in the fridge for 5 more minutes, then

turn upside down and tap individual cavities with a wooden spoon.

5. Store in a cool place, or in an airtight container in the fridge, bringing to room temp before opening up again to avoid condensation.

6. Share.

MOUNTAIN SPECIALTIES

The final chapter is a mixture of recipes that don't fit into other categories, but I knew deserved a spot in this book—and on your table.

RECIPES:

Apple Galette
Brisée Dough
Chocolate Pecan Bread Pudding
Sweetened Whipped Cream
Cream Cheese Wontons
Crunchy Chocolate & Nut Medley
Honey Vanilla Panna Cotta
Winter Spice Cake
Hungarian Pastry Cream

APPLE GALETTE

*I*n the United States, we love our apple pie, but there are endless versions of it. Apple and bread desserts have been around for as long as baking. Apple Galette is an old and rustic version, created before there was such a thing as a pie pan, tart shell, or a cobbler dish.

While it's French cousin Tart Tatin goes back to the 1880s, Galettes can be traced back to 15th century Italy, where they are known as crostatas and then adopted and renamed by the French.

I like everything about galettes, their look, the crispness of the crust you don't get in a pie, and their diversity. It's tough to get a galette wrong because they are imperfect to begin with.

BRISÉE DOUGH:

Ingredients:
    10.5 oz All Purpose Flour
    1 ½ tsp Granulated Sugar
    ¾ tsp Salt
    9 oz Butter
    ½ Cup 1 Tbsp Ice Water

Yield: Dough for 2 9" Galettes, Filling for 1 9" galette.
Time: 3 hours total
Tools Needed: Electric mixer or pastry blender, measuring cups and spoons, digital scale, rolling pin, sheet pan, parchment paper, cutting board, sharp french knife or bread knife, large sauté pan, rubber spatula, flipping spatula.
Pro Tips: This dough recipe can be used for savory galettes as well, just increase the salt to 1 ½ tsp, and replace sprinkling coarse sugar on top with seasonings or a little bit of coarse salt.
Altitude Adjustments:
Sea level-4,000 ft (and humid places): Start with just the ½ Cup of water in your dough.
10,000 ft+: Add water to your dough, 1 tsp at a time until you reach the right balance of moist, but not too glutenous.

Dough:

1. Stir the flour, sugar, and salt together.
2. Cut in butter until the pieces are pea-size.
3. Pour water all at once over dough and mix, stirring until the dough begins to come together.
4. Finish by hand so the dough does not get tough.
5. Portion dough into disks and chill for at least 30 minutes. For 9" galettes, weigh, and divide in 2. About 11 ounces each.
6. After chilling the dough, dust your work surface with flour and press your rolling pin into the center. Repeat this, rotating 3/8ths each time until the dough has flattened and softened some. Or you can bang on it, which is easier, but not everyone appreciates it.
7. Roll into rough 12"-13" disks, ⅛" thick. Mend any cracks and cut off any ends sticking way out. The beauty of galettes is you don't need a perfect circle. In fact, you want jagged edges, but you want the general shape to be circular, not ovular, and not looking like a strange continent with super deep bays and long peninsulas.
8. If your dough becomes tough and springs back when you try to roll it out, place it on a parchment lined sheet pan and in the fridge to rest. Then switch to rolling out the other disk.
9. Store in the fridge until 10 minutes before assembly.

FILLING AND ASSEMBLY

Ingredients:

2 oz Butter, cold

2 Tbsps Granulated Sugar or Vanilla Sugar (see vanilla ice cream recipe)

2 tsp Ground Cinnamon

¼ tsp Ground Cloves

¼ tsp Ground Nutmeg

4 Medium Apples, baking variety*

1 Tbsp Granulated Sugar

1 Tbsp Apple Cider Vinegar

Egg Wash

Coarse Sugar or Demerara Sugar for garnish.

1. Cut butter into ½" cubes.
2. Mix first tablespoons of sugar with the spices.
3. Cut apples in half down the center. Core. Slice apples 1/6" – 1/8" thick, best done with a very sharp french knife or bread knife.
4. Place the apples in a large sauté pan with a couple cubes of butter, the second measurement of sugar and the vinegar.
5. Cook on medium heat for 5 to 10 minutes, until soft and semi-flexible, but not totally cooked. This does two things. It evaporates some of the water out of the apples allowing them to shrink before assembly, so the crust is fuller after baking. Second, it makes them flexible for arranging in a tight pattern where some get curved or twisted.
6. Drain and catch the syrup from the apples. Cool the apples until safe to touch.
7. Pull your dough from the fridge. Make sure your dough is on a parchment-lined baking tray.
8. Preheat your oven to 375F.
9. Decoratively**, lay out apples on your 12"– 13" dough, in a super tight pattern. Keep the apples within an 8" diameter.
10. **Tip:** Use an 8" round cake or pie pan to make an impression in the center of your dough for a guide.Drizzle the syrup from the pan over the apples.
11. Dust with the seasoned sugar mixture.
12. Fold up your dough edges, pleating 7 to 8 pleats evenly

(roughly every 3-4 inches). Your raw assembled galette should be 8 ½" across, if not, tighten your folds.

13. Dot with remaining butter cubes.
14. Egg wash your crust, on top, and under the pleats, and sprinkle with crystal sugar.
15. Chill for 15 minutes.
16. Bake at 375F for 30-40 minutes. Some like to bake it in a 9" entremet ring for consistency in size, but it's not necessary and doesn't result in that rustic look.
17. Your galette is done when the bottom of the crust is golden brown, and the filling is bubbling. Check by gently lifting with a flipping spatula to peek underneath.
18. **Tip:** if the top of the crust is getting dark before the bottom is done cooking, lay aluminum foil over the exposed crust to insulate it.
19. Serve at room temperature with vanilla ice cream (found in ice cream and sorbets chapter) or whipped cream (see chocolate pecan bread pudding recipe on next page).

* Red baking apples, such as Rome, make a beautiful pattern of color for a galette. If you use tart baking apples like Granny Smiths, eliminate the vinegar.

A side note: If you are making traditional apple pie or cobbler with wedged or diced apples, you do not need "baking apples" at high altitudes. If you use baking apples at a high altitude for those applications, make sure to precook them or your crust will burn before the apples are cooked and tender.

** I like to lay the apples in a rose petal pattern, starting from the outer edge. Lay apple slices touching end to end inside an 8" circle. Repeat with your second circle directly on top of that, but offset the slices from the first one.

Your third circle will go 1/8th of an inch inside of that, and the ends will overlap by ¼ of an inch. Repeat this process until you have reached the center. Reserve more flexible apples for smaller circles. Your second to last circle will be made of two slices overlapping in a sort of yin-and-yang pattern, then your final slice will be twisted into a tight spiral. You should have some slices left.

The apples will continue to shrink as they cook, use these to fill in any spaces you see until you have a fully filled in finished product. Stuff as many in as possible, even making an entirely new circle in between existing circles if you can. You want them nearly standing up. If you've used them all and you think you can fit more apples in, take a fresh apple and cut some slices from that and stuff them in. Just make sure you keep the rose pattern look.

CHOCOLATE PECAN BREAD PUDDING

This recipe was inspired by a chocolate walnut bread pudding. Personally, I'm not a fan of walnuts. They are too bitter and acidic for me, but what I loved about that bread pudding was how it used melted dark chocolate.

Rich, creamy, flavorful, and the custard wasn't too eggy. I found a few chocolate bread pudding recipes. I tried to recreate that enjoyable mouth experience. Finally satisfied with what I'd made, I served it at my Dad's 61st birthday using challah bread I had made. I served it with vanilla bean ice cream (found in ice cream and sorbets chapter) and tempered chocolate garnishes (see page on tempered chocolate).

Ingredients:
   15 oz Dried White Bread
   8 oz Semisweet Chocolate, melted
   1 ⅔ Cups Pecans, toasted and chopped
   1 ¼ Cups Chocolate Chips
   10 oz Granulated Sugar
   ⅜ tsp Salt
   5 Eggs
   3 Cups Whole Milk
   1 Cup Heavy Cream
   2 Tbsp Espresso Powder
   Vanilla ice cream or whipped cream

Yield: Serves 12-16 people (closer to 16)
Prep Time: 20 minutes-1 hour depending on if your bread is already dry or not
Soaking Time: 30 minutes-1 hour
Baking Time: 1 hour
Tools Needed: 9"x11" pan or individual crockery such as french onion soup bowls or large ramekins, bread knife, sheet pan, medium to large saucepan, medium to large metal or glass bowl,
Pro Tips: The bread pudding will expand as it bakes, but as it cools it will shrink back down. Don't be afraid if there's a little overflowing.
Altitude Adjustments: Altitude really doesn't affect bread puddings, adding to why they are one of the easiest, yet most delicious desserts

out there. If I were to change anything for Sea level-4,500 ft, it would be to reduce the milk by 2 Tbsp because there will be less evaporation as it bakes. You should also do this if you live somewhere humid.

1. Cut bread into 3/4" cubes and allow to air dry overnight or dry in the oven at 150F for 45 minutes then cool for 15 minutes.
2. Spray 9"x 11" pan with cooking spray or brush with melted butter and dust with flour. Alternatively, use individual-sized french onion soup bowls and no spray.
3. Turn your oven up to 325F. Toast chopped pecans for 5 minutes once up to temp.
4. In a double boiler, melt the semisweet chocolate, or melt it in the microwave in 20 second intervals stirring in between.
5. Place the bread cubes into the 9"x11" pan or the bowls.
6. Sprinkle half of the pecans and all of the chocolate chips on top.
7. In a bowl, whisk together the eggs, sugar, and salt, then whisk in the milk.
8. Heat the cream and whisk in the espresso powder until dissolved.
9. Whisk the hot cream into the chocolate.
10. Combine with the egg and milk mixture. This makes your custard.
11. Evenly pour the custard over the bread.
12. Allow the bread to soak up the liquid for half an hour, then sprinkle the remaining pecans on top.
13. Bake at 325F until there are a few crispy corners on top and 145F internal temp. About an hour.
14. Cool for about 15 minutes to a comfortable, but warm, temperature of less than 115F.
15. Serve with vanilla ice cream (pg. c) or whipped cream (below).

∾

WHIPPED CREAM:

Cream about doubles in volume when whipped. One pint (two cups) of cream will make about 4 cups of whipped cream: enough for 16-20 people to get a good-sized dollop on their bread pudding, galette, pie, strawberry bowl, and more.

You can whip cream by hand with a whisk, but it's quite the work-out, and I avoid it for anything over 1 Cup of cream. If you decide to whip cream by hand, make sure not to hold the whisk like a pencil, but like a bottle with the wire end by your pinky-finger. Use your whole arm, not just your wrist. It may feel odd at first, but know that this goes for whisking anything by hand.

Ingredients:

2 Cups Heavy Cream, cold

2 Tbsp Granulated Sugar or Vanilla Sugar (See vanilla ice cream recipe)

1 tsp Vanilla Extract

Yield: 4 Cups (16-20 servings)

Time: 15-20 minutes

Tools Needed: Measuring cups and spoons, mixing bowl, electric mixer with whip attachment or whisk.

Pro Tips: This recipe has a very mild sweetness because the bread pudding is very rich and sweet itself. Taste it when your whipped cream is about 2/3rds whipped. If you want to make it sweeter, just add a couple more tablespoons of sugar, up to ½ Cup.

1. Combine all ingredients in your bowl.
2. Whip on medium-high speed until your whisk starts to leave a pattern.
3. Check stiffness, looking for medium-stiff peaks. Pull the whisk out of the whipped cream and invert it. Stiff peaks is

when the point stays pointing straight up, this means you have gone too far. You want your point to curl over just a little, but not relaxed completely. This is something that one of my chefs called "the DQ swirl."

4. Taste the whipped cream and add more sugar if desired.

5. Continue to mix and check frequently until you have the desired peaks. Be careful not to over whip; your cream will become thick and dense, and eventually break and turn into butter and butter cream.

6. Serve right away. Whipped cream can hold its stiffness in the fridge for up to an hour. After that, you may have to take your whisk and re-whip it a little, but this can only be done once or twice before the texture is ruined.

CREAM CHEESE FRUIT WONTONS

*E*ver since I spent a summer in Hawaii, my standards for Asian cuisine have not been satisfied. A week after I got back, I dined at a Thai fusion restaurant in my hometown of Park City with my parents.

Their Pad Thai was too sweet and their green papaya salad just didn't cut it, not when I had become accustomed to the fresh tropical fruit grown right there on the island. But I loved their cream cheese crab wontons!

I don't eat deep-fried food on a regular basis, but I enjoy it when I do. The combination of the fried crunchy shell and the sweet, rich crab cream cheese filling, plus the house-made sweet chili dipping sauce was addictive. I think I ate five out of the seven on the plate. I was surprised at how sweet they were.

If I didn't know there was crab in there, I wouldn't have guessed. Not sure if that's a good thing or not, but it gave me an idea. Cream cheese dessert wontons. So I googled it, and it turns out there are hundreds of recipes for cream cheese dessert wontons, but none of them had the fruit mixed in with the filling, just as a sauce on the side. So I made my own recipe.

These are perfect for bringing to a gathering with friends or pure self-indulgence.

WONTON WRAPPERS (OPTIONAL)

Ingredients:
   1 Egg
   1 ¾ Cups All Purpose Flour
   1 ¾ Cups Bread Flour
   ¾ Cups +/- Water
   ½ tsp Salt
   ½ tsp Granulated Sugar

Assembly and Frying Ingredients:
   48 2 ½" inch square wonton wrappers
   Water for sealing
   Medium pot with 2" of canola oil

as needed Powdered Sugar

Yield: 48 wontons
Dough Time: 1 hour
Fruit Time: 20 minutes
Making the Filling: 5 minutes
Assembly Time: 40 minutes
Frying Time: 5minutes per batch of 8
Tools Needed: Measuring cups and spoons, rolling pin, large bowl, wooden spoon, electric mixer, rubber spatula, digital scale, small saucepan, large pot, slotted spoon, sifter.
Pro Tips: Pull the cream cheese out of the fridge the night before. Don't limit yourself to just using the wonton wrappers for this recipe. Try making savory wontons, or ravioli, or chips. Stores in the freezer for 2 months if protected from drying out.
Altitude Adjustments: You may need a little extra water for your dough to come together at higher altitudes.

Wonton Wrappers:

1. Gather ingredients.
2. In a large bowl, stir all the ingredients together.
3. Knead into a smooth and workable dough.
4. Cover and let it rest for 30 minutes.
5. Turn the dough out onto a lightly floured surface and use a rolling pin to flatten the dough until it is thin enough to be fed through the pasta machine.
6. Flatten the dough with the pasta machine on the thinnest setting (setting 8 or 9 is good). If you don't have a pasta machine, split the dough in half and roll into 6" wide rectangles 1mm thick, adding flour to your work surface as necessary.
7. Cut the flattened dough into 2 ½" inch squares and sprinkle some flour on both sides of the wonton

wrappers to prevent the wrappers from sticking together.

8. Put the wonton wrappers into a plastic bag or airtight container as soon as possible to stop them from drying out. Store them in the refrigerator or freezer until ready to use.

CREAM CHEESE FRUIT FILLING

Ingredients:

1 8 oz Package Cream Cheese, room temperature

¼ Cup Mascarpone

½ Cup Granulated Sugar

1 Tbsp All Purpose Flour

1 Large Egg

1 Tbsp Lemon Juice

7 oz of Fruit. Apples, peaches, strawberries, raspberries, or black berries, cut into ¼" pieces

2 Tbsp Granulated Sugar

Filling:

1. Beat the cream cheese, mascarpone, and sugar together until creamy and smooth, scraping sides multiple times.
2. Add the flour and mix until incorporated, then add the egg and beat until combined, scraping sides multiple times.
3. If you are using a sweet fruit like red apples or peaches, add the lemon juice and mix until combined, if using tart fruit like raspberries or granny smith apples, exclude the lemon juice.
4. Cut your fruit into ¼ inch side cubes or pieces.
5. Mix with sugar and cook on medium heat, frequently stirring, until slightly softened.

6. Drain off excess liquid and save for a dipping sauce. Mix your fruit into the cream cheese mixture.

Assembly: See photos at end of recipe for assembly guide.

This is called a triangle ingot style fold, there are many other names for it: the swan fold, the Szechuan Chaozhou, the goldfish fold, and folding arms, but they are all pretty much the same. The positioning of the tips of the triangle in reference to each other varies a little, just find your personal preference. I like it because the pointed part is easy to grab for dipping in a sauce.

1. Set your square wrapper in front of you in a diamond position. Have a cup of water next to you.
2. Place ⅔ tablespoon of filling in the center of your wrapper square.
3. Take the corner nearest you and fold in half upward, making a triangle. Press air bubbles out before sealing shut with some water.
4. Next, lay a chopstick in the center vertically and make an indent.
5. Fold the left corner in. Add some water on top then fold the right corner on top of that, as if they were your wrists crossing each other with your palms up. Make sure they are sealed together, then move onto the next wonton. These can be stored in the freezer in an airtight container and thawed before frying in the future.

Frying:

1. Heat 1-2 inches of oil in a large deep pot to 385F.
2. Fry 6-8 of the wontons at a time for 5 minutes or until golden brown, stirring once or twice so all sides are cooked evenly. Remove from oil with a slotted spoon or a metal

sieve and place on paper towels. Repeat the process with the remaining wontons.

3. Cool for 5 minutes. Dust with powdered sugar.
4. Serve while warm with a fruit sauce, whipped cream (see chocolate pecan bread pudding recipe), or on their own.

CRUNCHY CHOCOLATE NUT MEDLEY

Photo By Cecelia McCarty

*J*f you like recipes that don't require perfect precision and you love delicious snacks, this is your recipe. Don't be intimidated by the number of words in this recipe. It's one of the easiest recipes in the book.

One day I realized I had all these partial containers of nuts and other ingredients leftover from previous baking or salad recipes laying around. We were out of healthy snacks, which is an emergency in this house, so I toasted and seasoned them and mixed it all together. I called it gourmet GORP, which has been officially renamed as Chocolate Nut Medley.

This was all improvised. Measurements and ingredients don't have to be exact. The important thing is that the proportions of chocolate to inverted sugar to solids are similar to the recipe below. There is ½ Cup+ of dark chocolate, 1 ½ Tbsp of honey, 4+ Cups of nuts, 1 Cup of shredded coconut, a handful+ of pumpkin seeds, and a handful of dried fruit, all well-seasoned.

Examples of substitutes:

- Honey: molasses, corn syrup, maple syrup, agave nectar, dulce de leche simple syrup, vanilla simple syrup. (Just make sure to adjust for flavor strength. The sugars are listed above from strongest to most mild in flavor and sweetness.)
- Shredded coconut: cereal, toasted sliced almonds, or toasted oats. (increase sugar if not pre-sweetened product)
- Pumpkin Seeds: sunflower seeds, pine nuts, or another nut.
- Sesame seeds: For sesame seeds it's about the flavor more than texture, so if you don't have sesame seeds add a ½ teaspoon of tahini or sesame oil.

Ingredients:

2 Cups Pecans, coarsely chopped

1 Tbsp Water, steaming hot

¾ tsp Sea Salt

2 Cups Peanuts, unsalted

1 Tbsp Water, steaming hot

¾ tsp Sea Salt

2 Tbsp Olive Oil

to taste Salt

¼ tsp Chili Powder*

2 Tbsp Sesame Seeds

⅓ Cup Pumpkin Seeds aka pepitas

1 ½ tsp Olive Oil

to taste Chile Powder

1 Cup Shredded Coconut, lightly sweetened

1 ½ Tbsp Honey, local

½ Cup Dark Chocolate, coarsely chopped

to taste, 3-4 dashes Curry Powder

2 dashes Cinnamon

½ Cup Dried Cranberries

Yield: 2 Quarts

Time: 90 minutes

Tools Needed: Measuring cups and spoons, sheet pans, parchment paper, flipping spatula, rubber spatulas, large and medium bowls

Pro Tips: If your nuts are already toasted and salted, just warm them up for a couple minutes at the end so they will absorb the chili powder and help melt the chocolate when mixing. If they are raw and unseasoned like mine were, follow directions below.

Altitude Adjustments:

Sea level-4,500 ft: Bake nuts for a shorter time.

1. Line two pans with parchment, and turn your oven up to 350F

2. Chop your pecans to the size of the peanuts then place in a metal or glass bowl.

3. Heat up 1 ½ Tbsp of water in a glass in the microwave until steaming hot. Mix in the first salt until mostly dissolved. Quickly drizzle onto the pecans and toss until evenly mixed.

4. Roast in the oven until you can smell the pecans. 5-8 minutes

5. Using a separate bowl, repeat the salt process with the peanuts.

6. Roast for 15-30 minutes pulling a tester out and allowing it to cool before tasting; every 5 minutes after 15 minutes. When done they will have a deep amber hue, a strong scent, and be crunchy when cool.

7. Pour hot nuts into the bowl and then add the olive oil, chili powder and additional salt. Mix until combined. They will absorb the oil and the flavor of the seasoning with it. Then add to the bowl of pecans.

8. Toast your sesame seeds until 50% colored and you can smell them.

9. To toast the coconut spread on a parchment lined sheet pan and bake flipping every 5 minutes with a flipping spatula until almost all are golden brown.

10. Once everything that needs to be toasted is toasted, mix them all together in a large bowl. Place the mixture back on the sheet pans and warm in the oven for 3 minutes. Return to the bowl and drizzle with the honey. Add the chocolate and spices.

11. Toss using wooden spoons or rubber spatulas. The goal is to melt most of the chocolate, so it coats everything and allows some of the mixture to stick together.

12. Lastly, add in the dried cranberries or other dried fruit.

13. Now you can enjoy this delicious and healthy snack or share it with your friends.

*Chile powder is generally not spicy, it is more smokey and earthy and adds depth and flavor.

HONEY VANILLA PANNA COTTA

This recipe, originally called *Panna Cotta au Miel et Vanille*, comes from the Balsam Inn in Montreal, Quebec, a spectacular Italian restaurant in the center of town.

In spring 2019, I did a five day *stage* there. I learned several homemade pasta recipes and techniques, their version of tiramisu, and other recipes. The Chef was kind enough to let me photograph all of the recipes I made and add them to my vault.

Every night after the guests left, at around 11pm, I got to try one of their amazing entrees straight off the line and enjoy a glass of beer with the sous chef as we conversed about our different experiences in the culinary world, (in English, as my French is mediocre at best). It was some of the best food I've ever had.

Leaf gelatin is the most common form of gelatin in Europe, and in professional kitchens. The advantage of it is a clearer result, a purer flavor, and no chance of unmelted granules. This recipe used leaf gelatin. But it is hard to find leaf gelatin in a US grocery store, so I have included measurements and instructions for both powdered and leaf gelatin.

. . .

Panna Cotta Ingredients:
- ½ Cup 3 Tbsp Heavy Cream
- ½ Cup Whole Milk or Almond Milk
- 1 Tbsp Filtered Water
- ¼ Vanilla Bean
- ¼ tsp Vanilla Extract
- 2 Tbsp 1 ½ tsp Honey
- 2 tsp (.17oz) Powdered Gelatin or 2 Leafs of Gelatin
- ¼ Cup 1 Tbsp Buttermilk

Glaze Ingredients:
- 1 Chamomile tea bag
- ½ Cup Water, steaming hot
- ¼ Cup Honey

24 raspberries or 6 medium large strawberries quartered into wedges

Yield: Four ⅓ Cup portions (7 oz. snifter glass), or three ½ Cup portions (12 oz glass)

Prep Time: 20 minutes

Total Time: 4 hours 20 minutes

Tools Needed: Saucepan or microwave safe bowl, rubber spatula, paring knife, measuring cups and spoons, and vessels for panna cottas: 7 oz glasses, molds, or ramekins.

Pro Tips: If you are using a saucepan to heat your liquids, make sure to scrape the bottom as you stir to avoid burning of honey or dairy. As a substitute for buttermilk you can use ¼ Cup of Greek yogurt or sour cream plus 1 Tablespoon of milk

Save the rest of your vanilla bean for our Vanilla Ice Cream (found in ice creams and sorbets chapter), Vanilla Sugar (see vanilla ice cream recipe) or Pistachio Mountain Rolls (found in breakfast chapter).

Use strong flavored honey for the panna cotta and a more mild honey for the glaze.

Altitude Adjustments:
Sea Level-4,000 ft: remove the ¼ tsp of vanilla extract; flavors can lose some strength at high altitude. Remove the 1 Tbsp water.

Panna Cotta:

1. Polish your glasses or pull out your ramekins.
2. Split the quarter of vanilla bean in half lengthwise and scrape out the insides with a knife. Store the rest of the bean in a sealed bag in the fridge.
3. Combine the cream, milk, water, vanillas and honey. Toss the vanilla rind in for infusion.
4. Heat on the stove to a simmer, stirring frequently. Or heat in the microwave in a glass or ceramic bowl for 3 minutes.
5. Meanwhile, prepare your gelatin.
6. **For Powdered Gelatin:**
7. *Sprinkle the gelatin into the hot liquid once it reaches a simmer.*
8. **For leaf gelatin:**
9. *Rehydrate your gelatin in ice water for 5-8 minutes.*
10. *Once the gelatin is rehydrated (soft and slimy), remove it from the water and squeeze out excess water.*
11. *Add gelatin to the hot mixture of cream, milk, vanilla, and honey.*
12. Stir until the gelatin and honey are completely melted and incorporated. If your gelatin clumps cook at a boil for 10 minutes, adding 1-2 tablespoons of milk afterword.
13. Whisk in the buttermilk.
14. Pass through a sieve to make sure there are no gelatin chunks left, and catch the vanilla bean.
15. Portion into 7 oz glasses, ½ full. Refrigerate for an hour. I used ¼ Cup of batter in 7oz snifter glasses, but ½ Cup works well in a white wine glass too.
16. For molds (metal or silicon), fill all the way and refrigerate for an hour, then dip in hot water for 15 seconds to release and turn out.

Glaze and Serving:

1. Infuse the water with the tea for 5 minutes. Squeeze as much out of the tea bag as possible without breaking the bag.
2. Measure ⅓ Cup of the tea.
3. Warm your honey before measuring.
4. Heat together until the honey is dissolved to make a simple syrup.
5. Spoon 1 tablespoon of syrup on top of each panna cotta.
6. Use any extra glaze to glaze your berries.
7. Serve cold with berries on top.

*P*ound cake gets its name from its history. In the 1700s, the recipe for pound cake was one pound sugar, one pound butter, one pound flour, and one pound eggs. No leavening agents like baking soda or baking powder, or whipped eggs, but they often included flavorings like vanilla, lemon or almond.

The lack of leavening made pound cake too dense. Modern pound cake recipes are still dense, but not as much as they were in the past, because they include leavening agents. This recipe, inspired by Hungarian cuisine, includes baking powder as it's leavening agent, and is flavored with some of my favorite spices.

You can use the filling recipe and assembly method below the main cake recipe, or find one of your own choice. This cake is also great cut into cubes and dipped in chocolate fondue, or simply served by the slice with a little butter.

Cake Ingredients:
    13.5 oz All Purpose Flour
    ½ tsp Baking Powder
    1 tsp Salt
    ½ tsp Cardamom
    ½ tsp Allspice
    ½ tsp Nutmeg
    ¼ tsp Coriander
    9 oz Cream Cheese, softened
    8 oz Butter, softened
    8 oz Brown Sugar
    8 oz Granulated Sugar
    8 Large Eggs, room temp
    1 Tbsp 1 tsp Vanilla Extract*

Yield: Two 1¼" tall 9" diameter cakes, or two 3" tall loaf pan cakes
Mixing Time: 30-45 minutes
Baking Time: 45-90 minutes (varies depending on altitude)
Filling: 20-30 minutes
Assembly: 20-40 minutes depending on how meticulous you are.
Tools Needed: Electric mixer, measuring cups and spoons, digital

scale, whisk, rubber spatula, large bowls, 2 cake pans or 2 loaf pans, parchment paper.

Pro Tips: If your butter is still cold when you're ready to bake, pop it in the microwave on a plate with a glass of water next to it. Microwave in 20 second intervals until soft, flipping the butter over each time. This allows the butter to soften all the way through with minimal meltage.

If your eggs are cold, put them in a bowl of steaming water for 10 minutes. The hottest your tap water will get is usually sufficient. Warm eggs and butter and cream cheese make a world of difference in the quality of your cake.

If the batter in your pan is deep, start the oven 25 degrees hotter than the recipe directs, then turn it down to the temperature stated for your altitude when you put the cake in the oven. This gives it a good oven-spring before things start to set and helps prevent caving in.

Variation: If you want to make this a vanilla pound cake, remove all the spices, increase the vanilla by 1 tsp, and replace the brown sugar with granulated sugar (totaling 1lb of granulated sugar for the 2 loaf recipe).

Altitude Adjustments:

Sea level-4,000 ft: Increase sugar by 3 Tbsp, baking powder to ¾ tsp. Change oven temp to 300F.

12,000 ft+: Decrease sugar by 2 Tbsp, baking powder to ¼ tsp, and bake with aluminum foil over the top to prevent burning on the surface before the inside is done.

See "What Makes Baking at High Altitude Different?" for more details on how altitudes affect cakes, quick breads and muffins. They are one of the most sensitive items in the baking world when it comes to altitude.

Cake takes a lot longer to bake at high altitudes because water evaporates at a lower temperature. It takes longer for the cake to reach the proper internal temperature to cook the eggs and gluten. This can cause cakes to end up more dry at high altitudes.

When assembling a cake in a high or dry environment, cut the skin off the top and brush each layer with a simple syrup flavored to fit your cake. Allow the cake to absorb the moisture for at least 4 hours before serving, preferably overnight.

Cake:

1. Spray your pans with cookie spray and line the bottom with parchment paper.
2. Whisk dry ingredients together in a bowl.
3. Beat cream cheese and butter until very pale and little tails have formed, scraping the sides and bottom often.
4. Add sugars and beat until fluffy. Scrape bowl well.
5. Preheat your oven to 325F.
6. Add Vanilla.
7. Add eggs two at a time, scraping the sides and bottom of the bowl in between additions.
8. Add flour mixture on low speed and mix until almost incorporated, but not quite.
9. Finish mixing by hand with spatula making sure to incorporate contents at the bottom of the bowl.
10. Portion into prepared pans.
11. Bake for 50-60 minutes, rotating pans after 30 minutes. The cakes are done when golden brown on top and a toothpick or paring knife comes out with just a few crumbs, and the cake bounces back if you press down with your finger. If you pull the cake out too early it will cave in and be gooey in the center.

∼

Filling and Assembly:

HUNGARIAN NUTTY PASTRY CREAM:

This recipe's technique is a little different than traditional French

Crème Pâtissière, but if you have made pastry cream before you will see the similarities.

Pastry Cream Ingredients:
1 Cups Sliced Almonds or Chopped Walnuts
½ Cup 2 Tbsp Confectioner's Sugar
½ Cup Whole Milk
1 Tbsp Cornstarch
1 Large Egg Yolks
½ tsp Vanilla Extract
1 Tbsp Golden Rum
¾ Cup (1 ½ sticks) Unsalted Butter, softened

Pastry cream:

1. Process nuts and powdered sugar in a food processor until the nuts are nearly a powder.
2. Pour the milk into a small saucepan and sift in the cornstarch. Whisk to combine.
3. Whisk in the yolks and cook over medium low heat, stirring constantly until it comes to a boil.
4. Continue boiling and stirring constantly with your whisk until it thickens enough to come off the whisk in a dollop (165F). And yes, your arm will get tired, so having a helper is great.
5. Strain the custard into a bowl set in an ice bath. Stir in the vanilla and rum and allow to cool to room temp, stirring occasionally.
6. Place your custard in the bowl of an electric mixer fitted with the whisk attachment; Mix on high speed for 30 seconds.
7. Add the butter one tablespoon at a time on medium speed, scraping the sides once or twice. Speed up the mixer for short periods of time occasionally to ensure smoothness.

8. On low speed beat in the powdered sugar and nut mixture.
9. Refrigerate with plastic wrap directly on the surface until stiffened and ready for cake assembly.

Simple Syrup:

½ Cup Sugar
½ Cup Water
½ tsp Vanilla

1. Cook until sugar is dissolved

Simple Icing:

1 Tbsp Rum
¾ Cup Powdered Sugar
as needed Water

1. In a bowl whisk all ingredients together adding 1 Tablespoon of water at a time until thin enough to brush with a pastry brush, but not too runny.

Assembly:

1. Level off one of your 9" cakes with a long serrated knife.
2. Brush your cake with simple syrup to add moisture if necessary.
3. Spread the filling all the way to the edges.
4. Place your second cake on top. Glaze with simple icing with rum added.
5. Place any remaining filing in a piping bag with a star tip and pipe a circle of 12 rosettes on top, one for each slice.

ACKNOWLEDGMENTS

A big thanks to everyone who helped me create this book. It would not be possible without the help and contribution of so many people.

I want to thank Griffin, my fiancé, and editor. If it weren't for him, I wouldn't have had the confidence to start this book, and it would still be just an idea. Griffin told me I was a pastry chef when I didn't think I was—and no one else seemed to think so either.

I ended up with great recipes and friends because I left my job of ten years to diversify my experience. He encourages me to get out of my comfort zone and feeds my need of travel and adventure. He made this book possible, spent hours going over words, structure, and photos, all for a smile and a kiss. Griffin is also a great taste tester.

I would like to thank my parents, they were a big part of the editing process, but more, they raised me to be the baker and pastry chef I am today. I am grateful to my dad for being my role model and teacher in the professional bakery at Deer Valley for over a decade, but really my whole life. And my mom was full of great feedback from a reader's perspective. My parents helped experiment with recipes and are professional taste testers too.

I want to thank my other teachers in the culinary world, in particular Tim Snyder, who fed my curiosity and growth the most when I had been at a plateau. Also, Heather Prine, Bobbye Sandman, Ryan Burnham, Oliver, Tom, Taylor, Caleb, and many more.

A big thanks to those who shared their recipes with me for this book. Diego, Florencia, Tim, The Balsam Inn, Hawaiian Crown Chocolate Co., Deer Valley, and my grandma Adrienne.

I must also say thank you to everyone who helped test out my recipes at various altitudes and took pictures. Cecelia McCarty, Grandma Adrienne, my parents, and Grace Foree.

Lastly, thank you, the high altitude baker, for picking up this book and sharing the love of baking in the mountains.

—Audrey Harty

CONVERSION CHARTS

Volume to Ounces to Grams of water		
1 Tablespoon = 3 teaspoons	1/2 ounce	14 g
2 Tablespoons	1 ounce	28 g
1/4 Cup	2 ounces	56 g
1 Cup = 16 Tablespoons	8 ounces	227 g
2 Cups = 1 pint	16 ounces = 1 pound	454 g
4 Cups = 1 quart	32 ounces = 2 pounds	900 g

Ingredients	Imperial Volume Measurements	Imperial Weight Measurements	Grams
All-purpose Flour, unsifted	1 Tablespoon	.33 ounces	10 g
	1 Cup	5 ounces	140 g
All-purpose Flour, sifted	1 Tablespoon	.2 ounce	5 g
	1 Cup	4.5 ounces	120 g
Cocoa Powder, sifted	1 Cup	2.6 ounces	75 g
Cornstarch	1 Tablespoon	.25 ounce	8 g
Powdered Sugar	1 Cup	3.5 ounces	100 g
Brown Sugar, packed	1 Cup	7.5 ounces	213 g
Granulated Sugar	1 Cup	7 ounces	200 g
	1 Tablespoon	.4 ounce	12 g
Butter	1 Tablespoon	.5 ounce	15 g
	4 Tablespoons=1/2 stick=1/4 Cup	2 ounces	57 g
	8 Tablespoons=1 stick=1/2 Cup	4 ounces	113 g
	16 Tablespoons=2 sticks=1 Cup	8 ounces=1/2 pound (lb)	227 g
Chocolate Chips	1 Cup	6 ounces	170 g
Large Egg	1 (out of shell)	1.75 ounces	50 g
Large Egg White	1	1 ounce	30 g
Lagre Egg Yolk	1	.65 ounce	18 g

Fahrenheit to Celcius Conversion Chart

Fahrenheit	Celcius	Fahrenheit	Celcius
-40	-40	112	44.5
-25	-32	145	63
-5	-20.5	160	71
15	-9.5	165	74
25	-4	193	89.5
32	0	200	93
41	5	203	95
50	10	212	100
65	18	250	121
85	29.5	300	149
90	32	325	163
95	35	350	177
100	38	375	190.5
108	42	400	204
110	43.5	425	218

Made in the USA
Las Vegas, NV
07 July 2021